MENTORSHIP AS A TOOL FOR SOCIAL CHANGE IN AFRICA

The Role of African government and Diaspora

Destino Nzonzidi Kazika

African Thought Freedom Press

ISBN-13: 9798882997174
ISBN-10: 1477123456

Cover design by: Destino Nzonzidi Kazika
Library of Congress Control Number: 2018675309
Printed in the United States of America

African Thought Freedom Press
Freedom House, Suite 4
123 Mandela Avenue
Lagos, Nigeria

For inquiries, please contact:
Email: info@africanthoughtfreedompress.com
Email: destinokazika@gmail.com

To the Unspoken Crisis in Eastern Congo

For over a quarter of a century, the eastern region of the DRCongo has been besieged by a crisis that has remained largely unspoken on the global stage. A silent genocide unfolds, marked by violence, displacement, and suffering that has touched the lives of millions. In the shadows of the world's attention, communities have been torn apart, and countless lives have been lost or irrevocably changed.

This page is dedicated to the resilient people of eastern Congo, whose stories of pain and perseverance are too often left untold. It is a solemn recognition of the hardships they endure and a testament to their unwavering spirit in the face of unimaginable challenges. As you embark on this journey through the pages of this book, let this dedication serve as a reminder of the power of mentorship, education, and community engagement as tools not just for personal development but as beacons of hope for regions ravaged by conflict. The crisis in eastern Congo underscores the critical need for concerted efforts to bring about peace, stability, and social change.

May this acknowledgment inspire action, conversation, and support for the Congolese people and all those facing similar plights around the world. It is a call to not only bear witness to their suffering but to actively contribute to creating a future where such atrocities are no longer a reality.

Together, let us commit to making mentorship and social change instruments of healing and transformation for the communities in eastern Congo and beyond, building a world where peace and justice prevail.

ACKNOWLEDGEMENT

Writing this book has been a journey of exploration, learning, and profound inspiration. It would not have been possible without the support, guidance, and encouragement of numerous individuals who have contributed to various capacities. I extend my heartfelt thanks to all of them.

First, I am deeply grateful to the mentors and mentees across Africa, especially those from SAYes Youth Mentoring in South Africa, whose stories and experiences form the backbone of this work. Their courage, resilience, and unwavering commitment to making a difference have been the true inspiration behind this book. Sharing their journeys has not only enriched this manuscript but also reinforced the transformative power of mentorship.

I owe a debt of gratitude to Dr. Andrew Dellis, the operational director of SAYes Youth Mentoring in South Africa, and Dr. Mandi MacDonald, a senior lecturer in Social Work from Queen's University Belfast, who generously shared their insights and feedback. Their expertise and constructive criticism were invaluable in shaping the narrative and ensuring accuracy.

My appreciation also extends to the various organizations and community leaders dedicated to youth mentorship programs in Africa. Their openness and willingness to share knowledge and resources have been instrumental in highlighting the impactful work being done on the ground.

To my editor, Arthur Wright, whose keen eye and sage advice have greatly enhanced the quality of this manuscript, I am profoundly thankful. Your patience and professionalism have made this a better book.

I must also thank my family and friends for their endless encouragement and support. To my wife, Naomi Ndongo Babo, who has been my anchor and source of strength throughout this process, your belief in my vision has been a constant source of motivation.

Finally, to the readers who pick up this book in search of understanding, inspiration, or guidance, I hope you find within these pages a spark that ignites your passion for mentorship as a tool for social change.

This book is a tribute to all who believe in the power of mentorship to transform lives and communities. Together, we can shape a brighter future for the next generation, not just in Africa but across the entire world.

CONTENTS

PREFACE

Writing this book has been a journey of exploration, reflection, and discovery. As someone deeply invested in youth development and now investing in the development of mentorship programs across Africa, I have witnessed firsthand the transformative power of guidance and support. This book is the culmination of years of work, countless conversations, and the shared wisdom of many dedicated individuals. My path into mentorship was deliberate, spurred by the realization of its power as a catalyst for positive transformation.

As I sit down to write this preface, my heart is filled with a mixture of emotions—gratitude, anticipation, and a deep sense of responsibility. Over the past 14 years, my journey through the realms of mentorship has been both transformative and enlightening. This book, "MENTORSHIP AS A TOOL FOR SOCIAL CHANGE IN AFRICA," weaves together my personal and professional experiences with the broader narrative of mentorship's potential to foster social change across the continent.

In Africa, where the youth constitute a significant portion of the population, the importance of mentorship cannot be overstated. The challenges we face are comprehensive, encompassing educational, economic, and social spheres. However, these challenges also present vast opportunities for growth, innovation, and societal evolution. This book is an exploration of those opportunities. It reflects on mentorship's capacity to inspire, empower, and unleash the inherent potential within each individual.

Writing about a continent as diverse as Africa is no small task. Africa is composed of 54 recognized sovereign countries, each with its unique culture, traditions, and challenges. In this book, I take the bold step of discussing Africa as if it were a single entity. This approach is not meant to diminish the individuality of each nation but to highlight the shared experiences and commonalities that bind them together. It is my hope that this perspective will provide readers with a deeper understanding of the collective narrative of mentorship across Africa.

The ensuing chapters delve deep into the essence of mentorship, uncovering its complexities and celebrating its beauty. This narrative is an invitation to explore the heart of mentorship, understanding its nuances and challenges, and recognizing its significant role in driving social change. Through personal stories of growth and broader discussions on the involvement of governments, NGOs, and the private sector, this book offers a comprehensive look at mentorship within the African context.

I am immensely grateful to the mentors, mentees, and community leaders who generously shared their experiences with me. Their voices are the heart of this book. I also extend my gratitude to the organizations and colleagues who supported this project, providing valuable feedback and encouragement. This work is dedicated to the mentors who invest their time and energy into nurturing the next generation, the mentees who courageously chase their dreams, and everyone who believes in the transformative power of mentorship.

As you turn these pages, I hope you find inspiration, gain insights, and most importantly, reaffirm your faith in mentorship as a pivotal tool for social change. The future of Africa rests in our hands, its youth, and through mentorship, we have a unique opportunity to mold a brighter, more prosperous future for all. This book complements my third book, "HOW IT FEELS TO BE AN ORPHAN: The Impact of Mentorship from Child and Youth Care Centre," where I share my personal stories.

Let this book serve as a call to action and a reminder of the profound difference we can make by investing in others' potential. Through mentorship, we can ensure that the seeds of change planted today will blossom into a brighter future for generations to come.

INTRODUCTION

Africa is composed of 54 recognized sovereign countries, making it the continent with the second highest number of countries, after Asia. In this book, I am taking the bold step of discussing Africa as if it were a single entity, even though I fully acknowledge the vast diversity and individuality of its nations. This approach might seem risky, but there is a method to this madness.

I am well aware of the rich tapestry of cultures, traditions, and languages that exist across the continent. Each country has its unique identity and historical context. However, there are also profound similarities and shared experiences that knit these diverse nations together. These common threads—whether they be cultural practices, social norms, or historical legacies—create a collective narrative that can be powerfully unified in the context of this book.

By treating Africa as a cohesive whole, I aim to highlight these shared elements and provide a more accessible and coherent narrative for readers. This approach is not meant to diminish the individuality of each nation but rather to emphasize the commonalities that can foster a deeper understanding and appreciation of the continent as a whole. It is an attempt to bridge the gaps between the diverse experiences of African nations, presenting a unified vision that resonates with the broader themes of mentorship, development, and social change explored in this book.

This unifying perspective can help readers, especially those less familiar with Africa's intricacies, to grasp the overarching dynamics at play. It simplifies complex interconnections and allows us to see the continent's potential as a collective force for positive change. In doing so, we can appreciate both the diversity and the unity that make Africa such a unique and vibrant part of the world.

Therefore, while acknowledging the risk, I believe this approach will ultimately make the book more meaningful and impactful. It allows us to celebrate the rich diversity of Africa while also recognizing the shared struggles and triumphs that bind its people together. This holistic view can inspire a sense of solidarity and shared purpose, encouraging readers to see beyond borders and appreciate the continent's collective journey towards a brighter future.

UNDERSTANDING MENTORSHIP IN AFRICA

Mentorship in Africa, often misinterpreted as merely a supportive relationship, actually represents a fundamental, culturally ingrained practice critical to shaping the continent's societal fabric and its future. This chapter aims to decode the historical roots and the profound significance of both formal and informal mentorship across the continent.

Historically, mentorship in Africa transcends the conventional frameworks found elsewhere, embodying a deeply rooted cultural norm pivotal in guiding the youth through life's complexities and instilling in them the values and wisdom of preceding generations. Unlike the structured mentorship programs prevalent in the Western world, African mentorship thrives on its fluidity and encompasses not only professional guidance but also the transmission of cultural heritage, ethical values, and communal responsibilities.

The roots of mentorship in Africa are as ancient as the continent itself, woven into the fabric of oral traditions and communal living that define many African societies. Elders, revered for their accumulated wisdom and experience, naturally assume mentorship roles, imparting knowledge through storytelling, communal activities, and rites of passage. This form of mentorship, though informal, is essential in fostering a strong sense of identity, belonging, and purpose among the younger generations.

In contemporary times, despite the challenges posed by globalization, urbanization, and technological advancement, the core essence of mentorship remains intact in Africa. However, its methods and reach have necessarily evolved, adapting to new socio-economic realities. Formal mentorship programs, often spearheaded by educational institutions, NGOs, and corporate bodies, are increasingly prevalent. These programs aim to equip the youth with necessary skills to navigate the global landscape but are designed to complement, not replace, the informal mentorship that continues to thrive within families and communities.

The value of mentorship in Africa cannot be overstated—it is a powerful tool for personal development and cultural preservation. It ensures that the values, traditions, and wisdom of Africa are passed down through generations, playing a dual role in a continent where the youth demographic represents both a significant challenge and the brightest hope for the future. With over 60% of Africa's population under the age of 25, effective mentorship is crucial for harnessing the potential of young people and preparing them to lead the continent towards a prosperous, united, and culturally rich future.

Understanding the unique characteristics and values of African mentorship not only helps us appreciate its potential to foster social change and drive development but also underscores its role as a vital bridge between the rich traditions of the past and the ambitious visions for the future. Through the lens of mentorship, we envision a future where Africa's youth lead in creating a continent that is both innovative and sustainable. This chapter will explore the depths of mentorship's impact on individuals and communities across Africa, highlighting how this age-old practice continues to shape the continent's destiny.

The Concept Of Mentorship

The concept of mentorship, deeply rooted in ancient traditions and continuously evolving, finds its origin in the lore of ancient Greece, specifically in Homer's "Odyssey". The character Mentor in the epic is not just a wise advisor but also a symbol of guidance and wisdom, a role underscored by the goddess Athena, who often disguises herself as Mentor to guide Telemachus, the son of Odysseus. This intertwining of divine intervention and mentorship in the narrative highlights the revered status of mentorship as a bridge between generations and a medium for imparting knowledge and wisdom.

The transformation of Athena into Mentor not only deepens the significance of the mentorship but also enriches its conceptual understanding. Athena, representing wisdom and war, chooses to guide young Telemachus during his father's absence, indicating the essential role of mentorship in navigating life's challenges and complexities. This mythological foundation underscores mentorship's enduring appeal and its intrinsic value in fostering personal growth and professional development across various epochs and cultures.

From its mythological origins, mentorship has branched into diverse forms worldwide, from the gurukul system in India, where students live with their teachers, to the apprenticeship models of medieval Europe, emphasizing the central role of the mentor-mentee relationship in learning and development. Despite the evolution of its forms and practices, the core principles of mentorship—guidance, knowledge transfer, and nurturance of potential—remain steadfast across different cultures and societies.

Today, mentorship encompasses both informal personal guidance and formal, structured programs prevalent in educational institutions, corporate environments, and non-profit organizations. These modern adaptations cater to specific goals such as career development, academic achievement, or personal growth, ensuring that mentorship remains relevant and impactful.

The story of mentorship is one of adaptation and continuity, a tradition that has been a cornerstone of societal progress and individual development throughout history. Its ability to evolve while retaining its core principles is a testament to its intrinsic value. Mentorship is more than just the transfer of knowledge; it is a journey of shared growth, discovery, and mutual respect, shaping the destinies of individuals and the future of communities.

Historical Perspectives Of Mentorship In Africa

Mentorship in Africa holds a rich, deeply integrated role across diverse cultures, transcending mere professional development to embrace a comprehensive nurturing of individuals within their communities. This holistic approach has historically been pivotal for societal cohesion and the transmission of cultural values and wisdom across generations.

African societies, traditionally communal and interdependent, have utilized mentorship not just as an educational tool but as a vital societal function. Elders, respected for their knowledge and wisdom, play crucial roles as mentors, imparting essential life skills and societal norms to the youth. This mentorship extends beyond familial ties, involving various community members in the upbringing and education of all young individuals within the society.

One of the hallmark practices in African mentorship is the rite of passage. These ceremonies, which vary widely among different ethnic groups, are structured programs where elders transmit important life skills and ancestral knowledge. These rites mark the critical transition from childhood to adulthood, equipping young individuals with not only practical skills but also a profound understanding of their cultural identities and heritage.

Oral tradition and storytelling are also central to the mentorship process in many African cultures, where literacy rates historically have been low. Elders use stories, proverbs, and folktales to teach moral values and social ethics, providing a dynamic and interactive learning process that allows the youth to engage deeply and personally with the lessons imparted.

Furthermore, apprenticeship models are prevalent, where young individuals learn specific trades or skills from master craftsmen or professionals through direct observation and practice. This one-on-one mentorship ensures the preservation and continuation of specialized knowledge and skills within the community, contributing to both economic and social development.

Despite the changes brought by colonization, modernization, and globalization, the essence of African mentorship remains resilient and continues to adapt. Modern mentorship programs, though sometimes structured more formally, still draw heavily on the legacy of traditional practices, emphasizing personal growth, social responsibility, and the importance of community and cultural heritage.

The ongoing evolution of mentorship in Africa demonstrates its enduring significance, reflecting a commitment to nurturing the next generation, maintaining social harmony, and preserving cultural identity across the continent. This dynamic blend of tradition and modernity ensures that mentorship remains a cornerstone of societal development and individual growth in Africa.

Formal Vs. Informal Mentorship

In the realm of mentorship, the distinction between formal and informal approaches highlights varied methodologies for fostering growth and sharing knowledge within professional and personal spaces.

Formal Mentorship generally involves structured programs explicitly designed by organizations to pair mentors and mentees based on professional development goals. These programs are highly organized, often with set objectives and timelines, making it easier for organizations to track progress and outcomes. Formal mentorship is particularly beneficial in promoting diversity and inclusion, as it tends to provide equitable access to mentoring opportunities across an organization. Structured programs ensure that everyone who signs up is paired with a mentor, thereby avoiding biases that may occur in more spontaneous settings. This method is especially effective in environments where developing leadership skills and succession planning are priorities.

However, formal mentoring can sometimes feel rigid or forced, which might limit the natural development of a mentoring relationship. If the pairing is not a good fit, it might lead to challenges in the relationship, necessitating awkward adjustments or reassignments.

Informal Mentorship, on the other hand, emerges naturally and is based more on personal connections and mutual interests. This type of mentorship is often more flexible, allowing the relationship to evolve over time to meet the changing needs of the mentee. Informal mentoring can start at any time and continue for as long as both parties find it beneficial, without the constraints of predefined objectives or durations. It's often driven by the mentee's initiative, making it a very personal and self-directed form of growth.

However, the lack of structure in informal mentoring can sometimes result in inconsistency and lack of clear outcomes. Since these relationships are not always officially recognized or supported by organizations, they might not contribute to formal career advancement as effectively as structured programs. Moreover, without formal recognition, the benefits of mentoring might not be as accessible to everyone, potentially leading to disparities in who receives these opportunities.

Ideally, the most effective mentorship programs blend elements of both formal and informal mentoring. This hybrid approach can provide the structure needed to ensure broad access and measurable outcomes while retaining the personal connection and adaptability that make informal mentoring so valuable. In practice, organizations might foster a culture that encourages formal mentoring relationships while also supporting the organic development of informal mentoring bonds among its members.

Each type of mentoring serves distinct purposes and offers unique benefits, and the choice between them often depends on specific organizational goals, the nature of the work environment, and the preferences of the individuals involved.

Cultural And Contextual Considerations

Cultural and contextual factors play a significant role in shaping the preference and effectiveness of mentorship styles— formal or informal—across different environments and societies. Understanding these nuances can enhance how mentorship is leveraged for professional growth and personal development.

Formal mentorship, often structured with defined objectives and outcomes, is typically favored in professional settings where career progression and skill development are closely monitored and highly structured. This approach is particularly prevalent in corporate cultures that emphasize clear hierarchies and role definitions. For instance, in many Western corporate environments, formal mentorship programs are integral to leadership development and succession planning, providing a clear pathway for career advancement.

Conversely, informal mentorship thrives in cultures that value personal relationships and lifelong guidance. This type of mentorship is more fluid and evolves based on mutual respect and common interests. It's common in cultures where community and extended family structures play a central role in social and professional life. For example, in many Eastern societies, where respect and hierarchy influence social interactions, informal mentorship might still occur within a framework that respects these norms yet allows for a more personal connection and mentorship that extends beyond the workplace.

Cultural norms significantly influence the preference for either mentorship style. In cultures with rigid social hierarchies and formal respect protocols, formal mentorship programs can help maintain these structures while still providing growth opportunities. In more egalitarian societies, informal mentorship might be more prevalent, emphasizing peer learning and less structured interactions.

Moreover, each mentorship style comes with its own set of strengths and challenges. Formal mentorship offers a structured environment that can be easily monitored and evaluated, making it easier to tie the mentorship outcomes to specific professional growth or organizational goals. However, this formality can sometimes stifle the personal connection and flexibility that many mentees find valuable in a mentoring relationship.

Informal mentorship allows for a more flexible and personal interaction, which can lead to deep, long-lasting professional relationships that extend beyond mere career development. These relationships often provide broader life guidance and support. However, the lack of structure can make it difficult to measure success and ensure equitable access to mentorship opportunities, potentially leaving some individuals without the support they need.

The choice between formal and informal mentorship often reflects a blend of personal preference, organizational goals, and cultural influences. For example, while working with SAYes Youth Mentoring, a formal program might provide a structured environment with safeguards and clear objectives. Moving outside this structure into an informal setting may allow for deeper personal connections and more tailored guidance but requires careful navigation of boundaries to maintain professional integrity and personal safety.

Ultimately, whether one prefers formal or informal mentorship often depends on individual needs and the specific cultural context. Both forms have their place, and many find that a combination of the two, adapting over time as the mentor-mentee relationship evolves, can offer the most robust support system for both personal and professional development.

The Importance Of Mentorship

Mentorship, particularly within the African context, is indispensable. It's a beacon guiding the continent through its unique development path, marked by rapid population growth and swift technological and social transformations. Mentorship in Africa is far more than a mere transmission of knowledge; it's a dynamic interaction that nurtures the potential of young minds, helping to cultivate leaders, innovators, and changemakers ready to tackle the continent's distinct challenges and seize its abundant opportunities.

At the core of effective mentorship is the development of leadership skills. For African youth, guidance from seasoned professionals and community leaders is invaluable. It equips them with critical leadership capabilities like decision-making and problem-solving, essential for navigating the complexities of their environments and for future roles in community and beyond. This nurturing is crucial in preparing a cadre of competent leaders who will drive Africa towards sustainable development and prosperity.

Mentorship also significantly fuels innovation and entrepreneurship, which are vital for economic growth and job creation across Africa. By linking mentees with industry knowledge, networks, and resources, mentors substantially boost their mentees' capacity to innovate and transform ideas into sustainable enterprises. This form of mentorship not only fosters individual economic empowerment but also stimulates broader economic activity, creating a culture of innovation that addresses many of Africa's pressing challenges.

The community aspect of mentorship in Africa enhances social bonds and strengthens communal resilience. It creates networks where knowledge, experiences, and resources are shared, not just between mentors and mentees but among peers. These networks are crucial as individuals face personal and professional challenges, ensuring that support is available and that no one has to face their struggles alone. The sense of belonging and community fostered by mentorship can powerfully counteract social isolation and fragmentation, aiding in the social cohesion necessary for collective action and development.

In educational settings, mentorship has proven effective in improving learning outcomes and bridging educational gaps. Mentors provide academic and career guidance along with life skills that complement formal education, particularly valuable in areas where educational systems may struggle with underfunding or overcrowding. This support helps students excel academically, pursue higher education, and make informed career choices.

Mentorship is also a potent tool for promoting gender equality and empowering women and girls in Africa. Female mentors inspire young women by sharing their experiences and strategies for navigating gender-related barriers. This gender-focused mentorship boosts the confidence and aspirations of female mentees and challenges societal norms that limit women's participation in various fields or leadership roles.

Beyond these developmental benefits, mentorship plays a crucial role in the preservation and transmission of cultural heritage and values. In many African cultures, such as the Xhosa community of South Africa, traditional knowledge and practices are passed down through mentorship. The "Ulwaluko" ceremony, a coming-of-age ritual for young men, is a vivid example. Mentors guide initiates through this transformative phase, ensuring the preservation of cultural heritage and values. They recount their own experiences and teach traditional songs, dances, and customs associated with the ceremony, helping mentees understand not just the practical aspects of the ritual but also its deeper cultural and spiritual meanings.

Through mentorship, mentees emerge as adults within their community, recognized as custodians of their cultural legacy. They gain a deep sense of identity and belonging, equipped with knowledge and values to navigate adulthood. Moreover, mentorship instills in them the importance of cultural preservation, preparing them to pass these traditions and values on to future generations.

The value of mentorship in Africa today transcends the typical mentor-mentee dynamic. It is a transformative force that nurtures the continent's most valuable asset—its youth—equipping them to face the future with resilience, confidence, and creativity. Thus, investing in mentorship programs and initiatives is not merely an act of fostering individual development but a strategic investment in the continent's collective future, laying the foundation for a prosperous and sustainable Africa.

In reflecting on the significance of mentorship in the African context, it's evident that this practice is not just a means of transferring knowledge but a vital element of the societal fabric across the continent. Mentorship in Africa is deeply rooted in the cultural heritage and communal values that define its diverse communities. This tradition, enriched by history and adapted to contemporary needs, plays a fundamental role in nurturing the intellect, spirit, and potential of individuals, particularly the youth.

The importance of mentorship in Africa is multifaceted. It spans from traditional forms, where wisdom and cultural practices are passed down through generations, to modern adaptations where mentorship bridges the gap between education and practical, professional application. This evolution shows how traditional and contemporary practices can coexist and enhance the process of growth and development within communities.

Mentorship in Africa does more than prepare individuals for professional success; it helps mold future leaders, innovators, and change-makers equipped to handle the challenges of a rapidly changing world. With one of the youngest populations globally, Africa stands at a pivotal point where the potential for growth and global influence is immense. Mentorship can harness this potential by fostering resilience, innovation, and leadership among the youth.

As much as mentorship is a legacy of the past, it is also a beacon for the future. It illuminates the path towards a prosperous continent where the capabilities of the youth are fully realized. The challenge now is to modernize and formalize mentorship practices to meet today's needs without losing the essence that makes them uniquely African. Adapting mentorship to the modern context involves incorporating technology, expanding access, and ensuring that these practices are sustainable and relevant. This modernization will ensure that mentorship remains a dynamic force for empowerment and development, helping to shape a more resilient and prosperous Africa.

THE AFRICAN CONTEXT

Exploring the concept of mentorship within the African context offers a fascinating insight into how deeply intertwined this practice is with the continent's diverse socio-economic, cultural, and historical landscapes. Africa's complexity, with its myriad cultures, languages, and histories, creates a dynamic backdrop where mentorship is not merely a method for professional development but a crucial societal pillar.

Africa's diversity is profound, marked by over a thousand languages and numerous ethnic groups, each with its own unique traditions and social structures. This rich cultural tapestry shapes the forms and functions of mentorship, making it a vital tool for community cohesion and intergenerational knowledge transfer. For instance, in many African communities, traditional forms of mentorship are often less about career progression and more about passing down essential life skills, cultural values, and community responsibilities. This cultural element of mentorship supports social cohesion by reinforcing and renewing communal ties and shared values.

On the economic front, Africa faces unique challenges and opportunities. With some of the fastest-growing economies in the world, the continent also contends with significant obstacles such as high youth unemployment and educational disparities. Mentorship, in this context, becomes an essential strategy for leveraging human capital. By connecting young individuals with experienced mentors, mentorship programs can provide the youth with the necessary skills and knowledge to navigate and succeed in their local economic landscapes.

Furthermore, the historical context of African nations—shaped by colonialism and the quest for post-colonial identity and development—also impacts mentorship practices. Historical influences have shaped social structures and educational systems, which in turn influence how mentorship is perceived and implemented. Understanding this historical dimension is crucial for developing mentorship programs that are not only culturally sensitive but also capable of addressing the specific needs and aspirations of African youth.

Mentorship in Africa, therefore, transcends the transfer of knowledge and skills. It is about nurturing the potential of young people and equipping them with the tools necessary for leadership and innovation. It is about understanding the nuanced interplay of socio-economic factors, cultural diversity, and historical contexts to effectively harness the continent's vast potential. This holistic approach to mentorship can pave the way for a sustainable future, where Africa's youth lead and innovate in ways that reflect their rich heritage and dynamic capabilities.

Socio-Economic Challenges And Opportunities

The socio-economic landscape of Africa, with its stark contrasts between bustling urban centers and serene but isolated rural areas, presents a complex array of challenges and opportunities that significantly impact the continent's youth. This diversity is not only cultural but also economic, affecting access to education, employment, and personal growth opportunities. The reality of these disparities can often lead to unequal opportunities, particularly for young people who are crucial to shaping Africa's future.

In many urban areas across Africa, there is better access to education and employment opportunities, which attracts a large number of young people seeking better prospects. However, this often results in overcrowded cities and either unemployment or underemployment, as the available opportunities cannot keep pace with the demand. On the flip side, many rural areas, while rich in tradition and community life, lack essential educational facilities and economic opportunities. This disadvantage leaves their youth unprepared and unable to compete in a rapidly modernizing global landscape.

Education in Africa varies dramatically from one region to another— some areas boast advanced educational infrastructure and systems, while others struggle with insufficient resources, a lack of qualified teachers, and limited access to technology. These disparities hinder the youth's ability to compete on both global and local scales, impacting their professional and personal development prospects.

Employment opportunities further complicate the socio-economic landscape. With a burgeoning youth population, Africa faces high unemployment rates, with formal job markets unable to absorb the influx of new workers each year. This situation perpetuates poverty and underdevelopment, especially in areas already facing economic difficulties.

Amid these challenges, mentorship stands out as a beacon of hope. Mentorship programs provide essential guidance and support, helping bridge the gap between the theoretical knowledge gained in formal education and the practical skills needed in the workforce. These programs play a crucial role in professional development and offer emotional and psychological support, helping young individuals navigate the complexities of their socio-economic realities.

Mentors use their experiences to guide mentees through the intricacies of finding employment, developing entrepreneurial ventures, or furthering their education. This guidance—preferred over direct advice as per the approach of SAYes Youth Mentoring—is more effective as today's youth tend to be more receptive to guidance, which empowers them to make decisions rather than just follow instructions.

Despite the socio-economic challenges, Africa's landscape is replete with opportunities. The continent's vast natural resources, youthful demographic, and growing connectivity offer fertile ground for innovation and economic growth. Mentorship can unlock this potential by fostering entrepreneurship, thus helping young Africans not only to find jobs but to create them, shifting from being job seekers to job creators.

Moreover, mentorship can help democratize access to these opportunities, ensuring that young talent from rural or disadvantaged backgrounds can receive the guidance and support needed to advance. By leveling the playing field, mentorship ensures that every young person can contribute to and benefit from the continent's growth, paving the way for a more prosperous and resilient Africa.

Cultural Heritage And Values

Africa's rich cultural heritage deeply influences its mentorship practices, shaping them into vehicles for not only professional growth but also ethical and communal development. The tapestry of African cultures, with its profound respect for community and elders, underscores a mentorship approach that extends beyond individual success to foster broader societal well-being.

Central to African cultural values is the concept of Ubuntu, which translates from Nguni Bantu as "I am because we are." This philosophy captures the essence of interconnectedness and collective responsibility that is prevalent across many African societies. Mentorship, within this cultural framework, becomes more than just personal guidance; it is a community endeavor where the growth and success of one individual resonate throughout the entire community. For example, in many traditional societies, the achievements of a young person are often celebrated as a communal triumph, illustrating the deep-rooted practice of shared successes and mutual support.

Respect for elders is another critical aspect deeply woven into the fabric of African mentorship. Elders are traditionally seen as the custodians of wisdom and knowledge, guiding the younger generation through complex life challenges. This reverence significantly shapes the mentor-mentee dynamics, where relationships are built on deep respect and trust, enabling a more profound and impactful transfer of knowledge. In many African cultures, such as among the Maasai of Kenya, elders teach young men and women the skills and cultural norms necessary for adulthood through direct mentorship and storytelling, emphasizing the transfer of sacred knowledge and community values.

Moreover, the way knowledge is transmitted in African societies often involves storytelling, proverbs, and folklore, which are not merely educational tools but also means to impart moral values and life skills. These stories are laden with lessons on integrity, perseverance, and cooperation, essential for maintaining the social fabric of the communities. For instance, in West Africa, griots (traditional storytellers) have historically played a crucial role in education and mentorship, using stories and music to pass down important historical and ethical teachings from one generation to the next.

Mentorship in Africa also places a strong emphasis on fostering individual integrity and moral character. This focus is crucial in a continent where many countries face challenges related to governance and social equity. Mentors strive to cultivate mentees who are not only professionally successful but also demonstrate strong ethical principles and a commitment to societal welfare. This dimension of mentorship is vital for developing leaders and professionals who can contribute positively to their communities and the broader African society.

The role of mentorship in Africa, therefore, is a testament to the continent's cultural heritage and values. It is a holistic practice that nurtures the individual, supports community bonds, and perpetuates the cultural richness that defines various African societies. As Africa continues to navigate its path towards socio-economic development, the foundational cultural principles embodied in mentorship practices will play a crucial role in guiding the continent's youth towards a prosperous future.

Historical Perspectives On Education And Leadership

Africa's historical landscape of education and leadership, rooted deeply in its diverse cultures and traditions, showcases a long-standing tradition of mentorship that predates modern educational systems. This rich heritage of knowledge transfer and leadership development has played a crucial role in shaping community life and governance across the continent.

In pre-colonial Africa, education was inherently practical and community-oriented. It was not limited to childhood or formal settings but was a continuous, lifelong process that every community member engaged in. Learning encompassed a broad spectrum of knowledge, from basic survival skills to complex governance and leadership principles. Elders and other respected community members, skilled in various disciplines such as agriculture, craftsmanship, and warfare, served as educators and mentors. This form of education was crucial for preparing individuals not only to thrive within their communities but also to assume roles of leadership and responsibility.

The role of elders in these educational systems was pivotal. They passed down critical knowledge and skills through direct engagement, storytelling, and observation, facilitating a seamless transition of cultural values and practical wisdom from one generation to the next. This traditional approach to mentorship and education ensured that leadership qualities were cultivated from an early age, with a strong emphasis on moral fortitude and community service.

However, the advent of colonialism introduced significant disruptions to these indigenous education systems. Colonial powers often imposed new educational structures that marginalized traditional ways of learning and leadership development. These systems frequently undervalued or outright ignored the rich tapestry of indigenous knowledge, instead promoting a form of education that aligned with colonial values and objectives. Despite these challenges, many African communities strived to preserve their educational traditions, adapting them in ways that maintained cultural identity and cohesion.

Following the wave of independence across Africa in the mid-20th century, there was a concerted effort to reclaim and revitalize indigenous education and leadership practices. Post-independence leaders and educators recognized the importance of integrating traditional mentorship principles with the needs of modern nation-building. This period marked a renaissance in mentorship and leadership development, tailored to forge identities and governance structures that reflected authentic African values rather than colonial imprints.

In today's globalized world, the challenge and opportunity for Africa lie in merging traditional mentorship practices with universal and modern educational frameworks. This blend aims to equip African youth with the tools necessary to succeed on a global stage while ensuring that they remain rooted in their cultural heritage. Modern mentorship in Africa is increasingly characterized by its inclusivity and adaptability, incorporating global knowledge systems without sacrificing the unique cultural and ethical foundations that have historically guided African societies.

Reflecting on Africa's mentorship traditions offers invaluable insights into the enduring power of education and leadership development that is deeply embedded in cultural values and community life. As Africa continues to evolve, these historical perspectives provide a robust foundation for nurturing future generations of leaders who are well-equipped to handle both local and global challenges, leaders who value wisdom, integrity, and a profound commitment to their communities. This ongoing evolution of mentorship not only honors Africa's past but also paves the way for a future where the continent's potential is fully realized.

Empowering The Youth Through Mentorship

Delving into the heart of Africa, where over 60% of the population is under the age of 25, it becomes clear just how vital mentorship is. These young souls are not just the future; they are the vibrant, pulsing present of the continent, brimming with potential that could shape economic growth and societal transformation. However, unleashing this immense potential isn't without its challenges—challenges like educational disparities, high unemployment rates, and the effects of rapid social and economic changes. In such a landscape, mentorship emerges not just as a helpful tool, but as a vital pathway to empowerment and active societal engagement.

Take, for example, the educational hurdles that many African youths face. Issues like inadequate infrastructure, insufficient quality teaching, and socioeconomic barriers often hinder their educational progress. Here, mentorship programs can light the way. It matches young individuals with mentors who have walked similar paths and emerged victorious, offering more than academic guidance—they provide personal insights and strategies for success. For instance, mentors can help mentees navigate educational challenges, provide career advice, advocacy, and support, and encourage perseverance through personal examples.

Unemployment looms large too, with many young Africans struggling to secure sustainable employment in overcrowded job markets. Mentorship here transforms from a mere support mechanism to a launchpad for innovation and entrepreneurship. Seasoned professionals guide these young minds, not just in job readiness, but in carving out new opportunities for themselves. This guidance often includes an introduction to valuable networks and resources, along with real-world skills that extend beyond the traditional classroom setting. By nurturing entrepreneurial spirit, mentorship encourages young Africans to stimulate their local economies and forge their own paths.

Amidst the whirlwind of globalization and technological advancements, the stakes are high. The rapid changes bring opportunities intertwined with challenges. In this volatile mix, mentors act as anchors and navigators, offering stability and seasoned guidance on embracing new technologies, tapping into global opportunities, and handling the complexities of modern life. This ensures that the youth are not just surviving but thriving in a world that's constantly evolving.

At its essence, mentorship is a form of empowerment. It's about building leadership qualities, instilling confidence, and fostering resilience among the youth. Through structured goal setting, leadership training, and strategic decision-making exercises, mentorship prepares them to assume significant roles within their communities and the wider world. This nurturing process is essential, cultivating a generation that values responsibility, ethical behavior, and a dedication to societal betterment.

In sum, pouring resources and energy into mentorship for Africa's youth is not merely beneficial—it's imperative for sustainable development. It tackles immediate challenges like education and employment while equipping young individuals to lead and instigate positive changes. Such initiatives don't just promise successful careers for the youth; they aim to harness Africa's demographic dividend into tangible, widespread benefits for the continent. Through effective mentorship, Africa's young generation can meet today's challenges head-on and seize tomorrow's opportunities, steering the continent towards a more prosperous and empowered era.

Fostering Equity And Connectivity Through Mentorship

Mentorship in Africa offers a dynamic approach to bridging the wide socio-economic and cultural disparities prevalent across the continent. It acts as a powerful equalizer, providing essential guidance and resources to those in less privileged environments and helping to connect diverse cultures and communities.

In Africa, socio-economic disparities manifest starkly between urban and rural areas. Urban centers are hubs for education and employment, drawing people from less developed areas in search of better opportunities. However, this often leads to overcrowded cities and increased competition for jobs, which the infrastructure may not support. Conversely, rural areas typically lack access to the educational institutions and economic opportunities that could drive development. Mentorship can significantly mitigate these disparities by connecting individuals from different backgrounds. Mentors who have navigated similar challenges can offer invaluable guidance, opening doors to educational and professional opportunities that mentees in isolated areas might otherwise never encounter.

Cultural diversity, while a strength of the continent, can also present challenges, particularly when it leads to misunderstandings or barriers to collaboration. Mentorship serves as a platform for cultural exchange, enhancing understanding and appreciation across Africa's varied social landscapes. This exchange not only enriches the personal and professional lives of those involved but also promotes a more cohesive societal fabric.

Furthermore, mentorship holds transformative potential for rural and marginalized communities, which often lack access to quality education and viable economic opportunities. Effective mentorship programs in these areas can provide the knowledge and skills necessary for fostering entrepreneurship and community development, breaking the cycle of poverty and enabling sustainable growth. This empowerment extends beyond individual mentees, with the potential to uplift entire communities.

Education and career development are other critical areas where mentorship can make a substantial impact. For many young Africans, navigating educational systems and job markets is fraught with challenges, from inadequate resources to lack of employment opportunities. Mentors provide a supportive framework for these young individuals, guiding them in exploring educational pathways, identifying career objectives, and acquiring the skills needed to succeed. This guidance is crucial, not just for individual achievement but for the broader goal of fostering skilled, informed, and capable future leaders.

Through mentorship, we can foster equity and connectivity across Africa, addressing socio-economic divides and cultural differences to build a stronger, more unified continent. This approach doesn't just support individual achievement; it strengthens community bonds and enhances societal resilience. By empowering the youth to overcome barriers and achieve their full potential, mentorship programs contribute to a cycle of positive change, driving progress and prosperity across African societies. This strategy not only uplifts individuals but also ensures a more equitable distribution of opportunities, paving the way for a more interconnected and prosperous Africa.

Cultural Preservation And Adaptation

Mentorship in Africa holds a profound place, acting not only as a catalyst for bridging socio-economic divides and fostering personal growth but also as an essential medium for cultural preservation and adaptation. In a continent as diverse and culturally rich as Africa, mentorship serves as a dynamic bridge that connects the past with the present, ensuring that the wisdom of the elders and the richness of traditional knowledge are preserved amidst the waves of globalization and modernization.

This preservation of culture through mentorship is critical, not simply for the sake of holding onto the past but because it underscores the importance of cultural identity in fostering resilient and vibrant communities. When elders and mentors pass down stories, practices, and insights that are rooted in their cultural experiences, they are doing more than just teaching—they are providing a sense of belonging and helping to cultivate a deeper understanding of one's place within the continuum of history and community. This process enriches the mentorship experience, turning it into a powerful tool for cultural continuity.

Moreover, effective mentorship recognizes the necessity of adaptation, guiding mentees in applying ancestral wisdom to contemporary challenges. This aspect of mentorship is crucial because it ensures that cultural preservation does not hinder progress but rather serves as a foundation upon which innovative solutions can be built. It instills a sense of pride and continuity, empowering young Africans to navigate modernity with confidence, equipped with knowledge of their roots and the adaptability required to thrive in a rapidly changing world.

For instance, in communities where traditional farming techniques have been passed down through generations, mentorship can integrate modern sustainable practices, thereby enhancing productivity while still respecting cultural methods. Similarly, in the arts, mentors can help young creators blend traditional forms with modern expressions, ensuring that local art forms evolve but do not disappear.

Through mentorship, communities across Africa are able to maintain their unique cultural identities while effectively engaging with the global community. This balancing act honors tradition while embracing necessary changes, ensuring that development is both forward-looking and deeply rooted in the rich cultural heritage of the continent.

In essence, mentorship in Africa is more than a means to an end —it is a vital mechanism for ensuring that the continent's cultural past is not only remembered but also integrated into its future. This approach helps create a resilient, adaptive, and culturally aware generation, ready to face the challenges of today and tomorrow with a firm grounding in their heritage, demonstrating the true power of mentorship as both preservation and adaptation.

Mentorship In The African Development Agenda

Mentorship plays a pivotal role in the African Development Agenda, particularly aligning with the African Union's ambitious Agenda 2063. This plan envisions a transformed continent—prosperous, inclusive, and sustainable—fueled by the potential of its youthful population. Here, mentorship isn't just a supportive component, but a central strategy designed to achieve these transformative goals.

At its heart, mentorship in Africa is about the transmission of knowledge, skills, and values that are crucial for both personal and professional growth. By integrating mentorship initiatives with the objectives of Agenda 2063, the continent can fast-track its development. These programs, when culturally informed and specifically tailored to meet the unique demands and contexts of African societies, empower young individuals to contribute meaningfully to their communities. They help cultivate a cadre of leaders, innovators, and entrepreneurs who are equipped and committed to driving change and advancing sustainable development across the continent.

Moreover, mentorship is instrumental in promoting inclusivity. It ensures that opportunities for growth and development reach young women, individuals from marginalized backgrounds, and those in rural areas—groups that often face significant barriers to access. This inclusive approach is essential for realizing Agenda 2063's vision of a united and equitable continent, where no one is left behind.

Integrating mentorship into the African Development Agenda can significantly unlock the potential of Africa's youth. It ensures that the continent's future leaders are not only skilled and knowledgeable but also deeply rooted in their cultural identities and committed to the collective well-being of their communities. Through strategic mentorship, Africa can build the human capital necessary to achieve a prosperous, inclusive, and sustainable future as envisioned in

Agenda 2063.

Concluding this exploration of "The African Context," it is clear that mentorship is indispensable for fostering development and sparking social change across Africa. This chapter highlights how culturally attuned mentorship programs can effectively tap into the continent's unique socio-economic and cultural landscapes. By customizing these programs to the specific realities and rich cultural heritage of African nations, mentorship stands out as a powerful force in empowering the youth. It bridges societal divides, weaves together community fabrics, and propels the continent towards its broader developmental goals. Ultimately, embedding mentorship within the African context ensures that it serves as a catalyst for nurturing a generation equipped to lead, innovate, and drive sustainable progress across the continent.

CHALLENGES FACING YOUTH IN AFRICA

Africa, with its burgeoning young population, stands on the brink of transformative growth yet is hindered by significant challenges that could stifle its potential. As the continent with the youngest demographic globally, the stakes are incredibly high, making the support structures for its youth not just beneficial but essential. This chapter delves into the various hurdles that African youth face today—barriers that are not just hurdles but can be catalysts for change if navigated wisely.

Educational challenges are at the forefront. Many African countries struggle with underfunded schools, a shortage of trained teachers, and insufficient educational materials, which severely impact the quality of education received. For example, in rural areas, children often travel long distances to attend school, which can significantly affect attendance rates and educational outcomes.

Economic challenges are equally pressing, primarily due to high unemployment rates among youth. The formal sectors in many African economies are not robust enough to absorb the influx of young people entering the job market each year. This situation is exacerbated by a mismatch between educational outputs and the skills demanded by employers, leaving many young Africans struggling to find work that matches their qualifications.

Social obstacles also play a critical role, with issues ranging from healthcare access to the impacts of socio-political instability. Health crises, such as the HIV/AIDS pandemic, continue to disproportionately affect young people, while political turmoil and conflicts can disrupt their lives and communities, often leading to long-term psychological and economic impacts.

In the midst of these challenges, mentorship programs stand out as beacons of hope. They offer more than just academic or career guidance; they provide a supportive framework that helps young people navigate these multifaceted challenges. Effective mentorship can equip young Africans with the necessary skills to tackle these obstacles head-on, fostering resilience and innovation.

Moreover, mentorship can help bridge the gap between the potential of Africa's youth and the continent's socio-economic needs. By connecting young people with experienced mentors, these programs help cultivate a new generation of skilled, knowledgeable, and motivated leaders who can drive positive change within their communities and beyond.

Through this exploration of the challenges facing African youth, it becomes evident that mentorship is not just a supportive tool but a critical pillar in ensuring a prosperous future for the continent. It is about transforming potential into capability, thereby securing a brighter path forward for both the youth and Africa at large.

Educational Challenges

The educational landscape in Africa faces a complex array of challenges that significantly hinder the ability of its youth to access quality education and, subsequently, viable employment opportunities. These challenges paint a vivid picture of the struggles involved in effectively harnessing the continent's demographic dividend.

One of the most critical issues is the inadequate educational infrastructure. Many African schools are plagued by overcrowding, which is a direct result of insufficient classroom space. This not only makes effective teaching difficult but also compromises the learning environment, reducing the quality of education received by students. The lack of basic amenities like desks, chairs, and even essential learning materials such as textbooks exacerbates this situation.

Another significant challenge is the digital divide. In an age where digital literacy is as crucial as traditional literacy, many African students find themselves at a disadvantage due to limited or no access to computers and the internet. This gap prevents them from acquiring digital skills that are essential in the global economy, impacting their educational and employment prospects.

The rural-urban divide further deepens educational disparities. Rural schools often suffer from the most severe resource shortages, including a lack of qualified teachers and basic infrastructure. The geographical isolation of these areas also limits educational opportunities, contributing to higher dropout rates as students struggle with long distances to school.

The issue of underqualified teaching staff across the continent is another pressing concern. Factors such as low salaries, poor working conditions, and inadequate teacher training deter skilled individuals from entering or remaining in the teaching profession. Consequently, many educators in Africa, despite their dedication and passion, lack the necessary training and qualifications to provide effective education.

Moreover, there is a significant mismatch between the educational curriculum and the labor market's needs. Many educational programs in Africa remain overly theoretical, with insufficient emphasis on practical skills, critical thinking, and entrepreneurship. This disconnect leaves graduates ill-prepared for today's job markets, where innovation and practical skills are highly valued. The absence of entrepreneurship education is particularly problematic in a region where self-employment is often a vital pathway to economic participation.

Addressing these multifaceted educational challenges requires a comprehensive approach involving governments, educational institutions, the private sector, and international partners. Investments in educational infrastructure, teacher training, curriculum reform, and technology are essential. Additionally, rethinking educational systems to align more closely with labor market demands and adopting innovative education delivery models, such as digital learning platforms, could significantly enhance both access and quality of education across Africa.

Overcoming these barriers is crucial for empowering the youth of Africa, unlocking their potential, and ensuring the future prosperity of the continent. By tackling these issues head-on, Africa can transform its educational challenges into opportunities for growth and development, ultimately leading to a more prosperous and stable future.

Economic Challenges

Our continent's economic landscape is characterized by a profound paradox: while the continent is rich in natural resources and youthful potential, it faces severe challenges with youth unemployment and underemployment, creating significant barriers to its development trajectory.

Youth unemployment remains a critical issue, with a large portion of young Africans unable to secure employment that matches their skills and education levels. This issue stems from several factors, including rapid population growth that far exceeds job creation, educational systems misaligned with current labor market demands, and an economic structure overly dependent on sectors like agriculture and mining, which often don't create enough jobs to meet the needs of a growing workforce. As a result, many young people find themselves in a cycle of economic disenfranchisement, contributing in some instances to social unrest.

One significant challenge is the mismatch between the educational outputs and job market needs. Many educational institutions across Africa focus heavily on theoretical knowledge, leaving graduates unprepared for the practical demands of the workforce. This gap is particularly evident in industries that require technical skills and hands-on experience, which are often undervalued or underemphasized in school curriculums.

In response to the limited opportunities in the formal job market, a substantial number of young Africans turn to the informal economy. This sector, while providing essential employment opportunities, often lacks stability and does not offer social protections, such as health insurance or pensions, leading to precarious working conditions. Although the informal sector can be a hub for entrepreneurial spirit and innovation, the absence of formal support and recognition limits its potential as a sustainable solution for youth unemployment.

Entrepreneurship represents a promising avenue for addressing these challenges, offering young Africans the chance to create their own job opportunities and contribute to economic development. However, young entrepreneurs face numerous obstacles, including limited access to capital, inadequate business training, and a challenging regulatory environment. To support these young innovators, there is a critical need for ecosystems that provide access to financing, mentorship, and business development services.

Addressing Africa's economic challenges requires a comprehensive approach. This includes overhauling the educational system to ensure alignment with market demands, fostering supportive environments for entrepreneurship, and investing in sectors that have a high potential for job creation. Additionally, policies aimed at formalizing the informal economy and extending social protections to its workers are crucial.

By tackling these issues, Africa can transform its greatest challenge—its underemployed youth—into its most significant asset, propelling the continent toward sustained economic growth and development. This transformation will not only empower young Africans but also contribute to a more prosperous future for the entire continent.

Social Challenges

Navigating the social landscape in Africa presents numerous challenges for the youth, which profoundly affect our well-being and ability to integrate into society. These challenges, from health crises to social exclusion, represent significant barriers to our development and future success.

One of the foremost social challenges is healthcare accessibility and quality. Many young Africans struggle with health issues that remain unaddressed due to insufficient healthcare infrastructure, especially in rural areas, or the high costs associated with medical care. Mental health issues, increasingly recognized as crucial to overall health, are often stigmatized and under-resourced, making it difficult for young people to seek the necessary support.

The continent also continues to face significant challenges with diseases like HIV/AIDS, malaria, and tuberculosis, which disproportionately affect young people. The COVID-19 pandemic has further strained these challenges, overwhelming healthcare systems, disrupting educational pathways, and halting economic activity. This has not only posed direct health risks but also amplified existing health disparities, complicating young people's ability to pursue education and employment.

Beyond health issues, social exclusion and marginalization severely affect vulnerable youth groups, including women, the disabled, and those in rural communities. These groups often find themselves marginalized due to a mix of cultural norms, economic barriers, and systemic biases that restrict their access to education, employment, and opportunities for advancement. For example, young women face gender-based discrimination that limits their educational and professional opportunities, perpetuating dependency, and poverty. Disabled youth frequently encounter both physical and social barriers that exclude them from mainstream educational and economic activities. Similarly, those in rural areas deal with geographic and infrastructural isolation, further limiting their access to necessary resources.

The intersection of these social challenges with economic and educational barriers forms a complex web of obstacles that young Africans must navigate. These multidimensional challenges not only affect their immediate quality of life but also their long-term ability to participate in and benefit from their country's development.

Addressing these issues requires robust collaboration among governments, NGOs, communities, and international partners. Efforts must focus on improving healthcare access, addressing mental health stigma, combating infectious diseases, and dismantling barriers to inclusion. Policies and initiatives that promote gender equality, disability rights, and rural development are critical to ensuring equitable opportunities for all young Africans.

Mentorship programs can play a crucial role in overcoming these social challenges. By offering support, guidance, and advocacy, mentors can help young Africans access resources, overcome barriers, and navigate their paths towards personal and professional fulfillment. Effective mentorship not only empowers individuals but also has the potential to transform the broader social landscape, fostering a more inclusive, healthy, and prosperous future for Africa.

The Impact Of Technology

The rapid evolution of technology globally poses a unique set of challenges and opportunities for Africa, a continent marked by stark digital divides yet brimming with potential for technological innovations to leapfrog traditional barriers. This paradox is especially pronounced when considering the impacts on the continent's youthful populace, who could significantly benefit from or be hindered by these technological advancements.

The digital divide in Africa illustrates a significant challenge. For many, especially in rural or impoverished regions, access to reliable internet and digital tools is not a given but a luxury. This divide encompasses not only the availability and reliability of internet connections but also the affordability of digital devices and the level of digital literacy required to effectively utilize these tools. The lack of access affects young Africans disproportionately, limiting their ability to tap into online educational resources, acquire essential digital skills, and participate fully in the burgeoning digital economy. The divide doesn't just widen the gap within African societies but also between these young individuals and their global counterparts, potentially stalling their educational and professional progress.

Conversely, the landscape is ripe with opportunities for significant technological impacts through innovation. Mobile technology, widely adopted across the continent, provides a robust platform for creative solutions in sectors such as education, health care, agriculture, and finance. For instance, mobile and internet technologies have the potential to revolutionize mentorship by connecting mentees with mentors far beyond their geographical limits, offering broader access to guidance and knowledge.

In education, technology can transform traditional learning paradigms. E-learning platforms, virtual classrooms, and digital libraries can make high-quality educational materials and instruction accessible to students regardless of location, removing geographical barriers that traditionally hindered those in remote areas. Similarly, for young entrepreneurs, digital tools offer unprecedented opportunities for business development and market expansion, providing access to financial services and broader markets.

The key to harnessing these opportunities is addressing the initial barriers of the digital divide and fostering comprehensive digital literacy. Efforts to expand internet connectivity, reduce the cost of digital access, and incorporate digital skills into standard curricula are vital. Such initiatives require collaboration among governments, the private sector, and international organizations to build supportive infrastructure and policies promoting digital inclusion and innovation.

Moreover, the application of technology in fields like mentorship and education must be thoughtfully tailored to local contexts. Solutions should be designed with an understanding of the specific needs, languages, and cultural nuances of their intended users to ensure effectiveness and adoption.

The interplay of technology with Africa's socio-economic landscape highlights both the existing barriers and the transformative possibilities. As Africa moves towards greater digital inclusion, the potential for technology to redefine the boundaries of education, mentorship, and entrepreneurship is immense. With targeted strategies to bridge the digital divide and leverage technological innovation, technology can indeed become a pivotal force in empowering African youth, driving progress, and shaping a more prosperous future for the continent.

The Role Of Mentorship In Addressing Youth Challenges

Mentorship emerges as a transformative tool in tackling the multitude of challenges that African youth face today, ranging from educational and economic barriers to social exclusion and the digital divide.

In the realm of education, mentorship provides personalized support, guidance, and advocacy, crucial for bridging the gap between theoretical knowledge and practical workplace skills. By offering insights into various industries and facilitating hands-on experiences, mentors help youth navigate the complexities of academic and career planning. Successful mentorship programs enhance educational outcomes, highlighting the importance of role models who inspire continuous learning and higher educational aspirations.

Economically, mentorship addresses critical issues like youth unemployment and underemployment by connecting young people with experienced professionals and entrepreneurs. This networking provides valuable insights into the job market, equipping mentees with necessary job-seeking skills and entrepreneurial knowledge. Mentorship enriches professional development, enhancing essential soft skills that are pivotal in the job market.

On the social front, mentorship programs create supportive networks that help young individuals tackle social exclusion and marginalization. These programs offer a platform for discussing personal and societal challenges and developing coping strategies. By promoting community service and leadership development, mentorship encourages youth to take active roles in their communities, fostering inclusivity and positive social change.

Furthermore, in the digital realm, mentorship can significantly impact bridging the technology gap. Programs that integrate digital skills training prepare young Africans for the digital economy, providing them with the necessary tools to succeed in a globalized world. Online platforms extend the reach of mentorship, connecting mentees with mentors across geographic and socioeconomic barriers, democratizing access to knowledge and opportunity.

Thus, mentorship not only addresses immediate personal and professional challenges but also plays a crucial role in broader societal development. By nurturing a generation equipped to navigate and shape the future, mentorship programs ensure that Africa's youth can contribute effectively to the continent's growth and prosperity. As Africa navigates its developmental path, integrating mentorship into strategic planning is essential for empowering its youth and leveraging their potential to drive sustainable progress.

Reflecting on the diverse challenges faced by Africa's youth, it becomes evident that these obstacles, while formidable, are certainly not insurmountable. Mentorship emerges as a vital tool in this landscape, offering a beacon of hope and a practical pathway through the complexities of educational, economic, social, and technological challenges that young Africans encounter.

The profound impact of mentorship extends beyond individual success; it is crucial for nurturing the vast potential of Africa's youthful population. This potential is Africa's most significant asset for future growth, but without proper guidance and support, there is a risk that this potential could go unrealized. Mentorship provides the necessary framework to transform potential into success, making it an indispensable strategy for development.

From the educational perspective, mentorship bridges the gap between theoretical knowledge and practical application, equipping young people with the skills needed to thrive in both local and global job markets. Economically, it introduces young individuals to networks and opportunities that can lead to meaningful employment and entrepreneurship, crucial in a continent with high rates of youth unemployment.

Socially, mentorship helps navigate the complex social fabrics and cultural dynamics that could otherwise hinder young people from fully participating in their communities. Moreover, in the digital realm, mentorship supports young people in acquiring necessary digital skills, ensuring they are not left behind in an increasingly digital world.

The conclusion drawn from this exploration is clear: there is a critical need to enhance and expand mentorship initiatives across Africa. By cultivating environments where mentorship can thrive, we set the foundation for a future filled with opportunities. This means not only recognizing the potential of Africa's youth but actively investing in mechanisms like mentorship to fully harness this potential.

Such investments should be strategically tailored to meet the unique needs of Africa's young people, incorporating local contexts and cultural sensitivities to ensure relevance and effectiveness. As we look to the future, the focus should be on scaling up mentorship initiatives that can drive substantial and sustainable change, ensuring that Africa's youth can lead the charge in fostering a continent that is prosperous, resilient, and dynamic.

In essence, mentorship should not be seen merely as a support mechanism for individual growth but as a cornerstone of a broader developmental strategy for the entire continent. It promises not only a brighter future for young Africans but for Africa as a whole, highlighting the transformative power of investing in the next generation.

GUIDING EDUCATIONAL PATHS AND CAREER CHOICES

In Africa, the decision to pursue a particular educational path or career is fraught with significant implications—not just for individual fulfillment, but also for broader community impact and personal prospects. In this context, mentorship assumes a pivotal role, guiding Africa's youth through the complexities of academic and professional decision-making.

Navigating the terrain of educational and career choices in Africa presents unique challenges due to limited access to resources, information, and guidance. This situation underscores the invaluable role of mentorship, which becomes a critical lifeline for young individuals seeking to illuminate their potential paths forward. Mentorship offers more than guidance—it inspires ambition and provides the tangible support needed to make informed decisions that align with both personal aspirations and practical realities.

Mentors serve as vital navigators in this journey, helping mentees explore various fields, understand their passions, and reconcile these interests with viable career opportunities. This process is deeply influenced by the socio-economic and cultural contexts of the continent, where traditional values often intersect with modern career landscapes. For instance, a mentor can help a young mentee from a rural background understand and navigate the requisites for entering a tech-driven profession, bridging traditional expectations with contemporary economic needs.

The power of mentorship in shaping educational and career trajectories is profound. It not only guides young individuals towards achieving their personal goals but also equips them to contribute effectively to their communities and the continent at large. Through mentorship, mentees gain insights into the practical aspects of their chosen fields, from academic requirements to industry demands, which are crucial for making informed decisions.

This chapter delves into how mentorship can transform the educational and career prospects of African youth, turning aspirations into attainable goals. It highlights the dual role of mentors: as catalysts for personal achievement and as architects of broader social impact. In guiding the youth of Africa, mentors not only facilitate personal success but also foster the development of the continent, making mentorship an invaluable investment in the future of Africa.

Role Of Mentors In Academic Achievement

Mentorship is vital in enhancing academic achievement among Africa's youth, who face myriad educational barriers due to resource constraints and systemic challenges. By stepping in as mentors, experienced individuals provide not just academic guidance but also essential support that helps mentees navigate the complexities of educational environments and opportunities, laying a foundation for success in their studies and future careers.

Mentors primarily offer academic support, guidance, and advocacy helping mentees pinpoint their interests and strengths, which is essential for setting achievable educational goals. This support includes guiding on course selections, effective study habits, and potential career paths that align with the mentees' abilities and aspirations. This role is crucial, particularly in areas where educational support systems may be insufficient, allowing mentors to fill significant gaps. Personalized attention from mentors can be transformative, offering motivation and resources that cater specifically to the mentees' needs.

Moreover, mentors assist in navigating scholarships, internships, and other critical opportunities. Many young Africans lack awareness of the full range of educational opportunities available, both locally and abroad. Mentors play a key role in bridging this information gap, aiding mentees in identifying and applying for scholarships, preparing for interviews, and securing internships that provide valuable professional exposure and experience. These activities are crucial for integrating theoretical knowledge with practical application, enhancing the mentees' academic and professional profiles.

Mentorship also extends its impact by fostering broader academic and cultural exposure through guiding mentees towards participating in academic competitions and attending conferences, which enriches their educational experience and personal development.

The influence of mentorship on academic success not only benefits the individual mentees but also permeates their communities, fostering a culture of academic excellence. Those who have benefited from mentorship often become mentors themselves, perpetuating a cycle of support and success. This cascade effect can transform entire communities by elevating the importance of education and creating an environment where academic achievements are supported and celebrated.

In addressing systemic educational challenges such as high dropout rates and inequality, targeted mentorship programs can provide crucial support to at-risk students, ensuring a higher rate of educational completion and a more equitable educational landscape.

In essence, the role of mentors is integral to not only guiding individual students through their educational journeys but also to inspiring and cultivating a generation equipped to lead and innovate. Investing in robust mentorship programs is essential for nurturing a well-educated, empowered youth capable of driving socio-economic growth across the continent. This makes mentorship an indispensable strategy for personal development as well as a cornerstone for broader socio-economic development in Africa.

Career Guidance And Professional Development

In today's rapidly changing professional landscape, career guidance and professional development are more crucial than ever, especially for Africa's burgeoning youth population. With a significant segment of the continent's demographic under 25, there is a pressing need to steer these young individuals towards successful and rewarding career paths. Here, the role of mentors becomes indispensable, offering not just guidance but a roadmap for navigating the complexities of career planning and growth.

Mentors play a vital role in the first steps of a mentee's career journey, which typically involves exploring various career options. This stage is foundational, helping mentees understand the landscape of potential careers, including both traditional roles and emerging fields like renewable energy, digital technology, and agribusiness. These sectors are especially pertinent to Africa's development and offer new opportunities for economic growth and innovation. Mentors, with their depth of experience and industry knowledge, are uniquely positioned to illuminate these paths, helping mentees align their personal passions with professional opportunities that also serve broader societal needs.

Once a career path is chosen, the focus shifts to skill development. Mentors are pivotal in this phase, not just for imparting technical knowledge but also for helping to build a well-rounded skill set. This includes critical thinking, communication, leadership, and adaptability—skills that are indispensable in today's job market. Mentors can guide mentees toward resources for refining these skills, such as specific training programs and experiential learning opportunities. Importantly, mentors also play a key role in developing soft skills, which are crucial for navigating the workplace effectively.

Another critical aspect of professional development is networking. Building a strong professional network can open a world of opportunities, providing industry insights and facilitating strategic collaborations. Mentors can introduce mentees to valuable contacts and teach them the nuances of effective networking, such as how to maintain a professional online presence and engage constructively at industry events.

Moreover, understanding the norms and expectations of one's chosen industry can greatly enhance a mentee's ability to navigate their field successfully. Mentors provide insights into the cultural nuances and unwritten rules of industries, helping mentees adapt and thrive within their professional environments.

The comprehensive role of mentorship in career guidance extends beyond individual success; it is integral to cultivating a skilled workforce that can propel Africa's socio-economic development forward. By assisting mentees in exploring viable career paths, enhancing their skills, expanding their professional networks, and understanding their industry's landscape, mentors equip young Africans with the tools they need to succeed in a dynamic global market. This mentorship is not just about fostering individual achievement; it's about shaping a generation capable of driving progress and innovation across the continent.

Overcoming Barriers To Education And Employment

Overcoming barriers to education and employment is crucial for achieving equitable development in Africa, particularly given the significant obstacles faced by the continent's youth. This demographic, while representing a potential powerhouse for economic growth and innovation, frequently encounters challenges in accessing quality education and meaningful employment. These hurdles are even more pronounced for specific groups, such as young women and those from disadvantaged backgrounds, highlighting the need for targeted interventions. Mentorship stands out as a critical strategy in this context, providing tailored guidance and support to help navigate and overcome these barriers.

Gender disparities in access to education and employment remain stark in many parts of Africa. Young women and girls often face a range of societal, cultural, and economic barriers that impede their educational and professional progress. These include gender-based discrimination, cultural norms that favor male education, safety concerns, and disproportionate responsibilities like early marriage and domestic duties. Mentorship programs designed to empower young women can significantly impact these issues. By connecting them with mentors who have faced similar barriers and succeeded, these programs not only provide practical career and academic guidance but also offer powerful role models and advocates.

Successful initiatives focus on building self-esteem, leadership skills, and key competencies while providing practical support such as scholarships and internships. Workshops on rights awareness, negotiation skills, and financial literacy are also critical. These efforts do not just help individual young women; they also challenge and gradually shift the societal norms underpinning gender disparities.

Furthermore, mentorship can effectively support other vulnerable populations, including individuals from low socioeconomic backgrounds, those with disabilities, or living in remote areas. These groups often lack essential resources, information, and support networks needed to succeed academically and professionally. Comprehensive mentorship programs address these gaps by providing not just academic tutoring and career advice but also psychosocial support to boost self-worth and motivation.

For example, mentorship that includes identifying and applying for financial aid, vocational training, and facilitating internships can be transformative. In rural areas, mentorship might focus on agripreneurship and sustainable farming techniques, tapping into the local agricultural potential. Additionally, leveraging technology through digital platforms can provide remote mentorship, connecting mentees with global mentors and online educational resources, thus broadening their learning opportunities and access to professional networks.

The multifaceted challenges of education and employment in Africa demand nuanced solutions that mentorship programs are particularly well-suited to provide. By offering personalized support and leveraging the insights and networks of experienced professionals, mentorship can dismantle significant barriers facing African youth. This strategic approach not only empowers individuals but also contributes to broader societal and economic development, ensuring a more inclusive and prosperous future for all. Through targeted mentorship, Africa can harness the full potential of its youth, turning demographic challenges into opportunities for growth and innovation.

The Future Of Work In Africa

The future of work in Africa is poised at a transformative juncture, characterized by both significant challenges and tremendous opportunities. As the continent undergoes rapid economic and technological changes, the emerging job market demands a workforce that is skilled, adaptable, and innovative. Mentorship plays an essential role in equipping African youth with the necessary tools to navigate this evolving landscape effectively.

The job market in Africa is transforming, driven by technological advancements, demographic changes, and globalization. Key sectors such as technology, renewable energy, agriculture, and healthcare are expected to expand, offering new avenues for employment and entrepreneurship. To capitalize on these opportunities, African youth need more than just technical skills; they require a deep understanding of market dynamics and the capacity to innovate and respond to new challenges.

Mentorship bridges the gap between traditional education and real-world market demands. Experienced mentors provide invaluable insights into emerging industries, guiding mentees towards careers that are not only in demand but also crucial for the continent's development. They highlight necessary skills and competencies, encourage entrepreneurial thinking, and help mentees understand the broader economic and social impact of their career choices.

With the job market's constant evolution, the ability to continuously learn and adapt is paramount. Mentorship cultivates a lifelong learning mindset, emphasizing the importance of curiosity, open-mindedness, and resilience. Mentors help mentees develop flexible learning paths that include both formal education and alternative learning opportunities like online courses and workshops, ensuring they remain competitive and relevant.

Additionally, mentors exemplify adaptability by sharing their personal experiences with career transitions, technology adoption, and overcoming professional challenges. This guidance is crucial for mentees to view changes and challenges as opportunities for personal and professional growth.

Beyond individual success, mentorship contributes significantly to broader economic outcomes by fostering a generation of well-prepared, skilled young professionals who can drive innovation and growth. As Africa seeks to harness its demographic dividend, the strategic role of mentorship in developing a robust, dynamic workforce cannot be overstated. Mentors instill not only technical skills but also critical soft skills like problem-solving, leadership, and emotional intelligence, which are vital in today's global economy.

In sum, the future of work in Africa offers a landscape rich with potential but fraught with challenges. Mentorship is pivotal in this context, providing a foundational support system that prepares young Africans to thrive in dynamic and competitive environments. By enhancing their adaptability, broadening their understanding of emerging market needs, and fostering a culture of continuous improvement and innovation, mentorship programs play a crucial role in shaping the continent's workforce readiness and overall economic trajectory. Through effective mentorship, Africa's youth are not just preparing for the future; they are actively shaping it, promising a more prosperous and resilient continent.

As we reflect on the vital role of mentorship in shaping the educational and career trajectories of Africa's youth, it becomes clear that these relationships are transformative. Navigating the journey from education to employment is laden with challenges, but mentorship provides a guiding light, offering support and direction to young individuals striving to find their path. This exploration has highlighted the essential role of mentorship in helping young Africans understand and maneuver through the complex landscapes of academia and professional life, enabling them to make choices that are not only well-informed but also aligned with their personal aspirations and the demands of the market.

The need to strengthen mentorship programs across Africa is both urgent and profound. Such initiatives are crucial for developing a generation that is prepared to lead and innovate. Mentorship bridges crucial knowledge gaps, builds confidence, and opens doors to opportunities that might otherwise be inaccessible. Through these programs, experienced professionals can impart wisdom and insights, acting as role models and catalysts for growth and success.

Looking forward, as Africa continues to progress and transform, the investment in robust mentorship programs will yield significant dividends. The continent's future is largely in the hands of its young population. By equipping these young minds with the necessary tools, knowledge, and support through mentorship, we can foster a future that is not only prosperous but also innovative and led by well-prepared leaders. Mentorship is more than just guidance; it's a foundational commitment to the advancement of the continent, ensuring that the next generation can build a brighter, more dynamic Africa. This commitment to mentorship will undoubtedly play a pivotal role in shaping the future of Africa, making it a key strategy for anyone invested in the continent's long-term success and resilience.

PROMOTING HEALTH AND WELL-BEING

The importance of health and well-being in achieving personal and professional success cannot be overstated, especially for Africa's youth, poised to shape the continent's future. As we explore the essential role of mentorship in this chapter, it's clear that supporting the physical and mental health of young Africans goes beyond traditional educational and career guidance. Mentorship, with its broad potential, becomes a vital tool for nurturing healthier, more resilient communities.

In Africa, where the young demographic dominates, maintaining good health is foundational for realizing the vast potential of the youth. However, challenges abound, from mental health and stress management to sexual health and lifestyle choices, often exacerbated by limited access to health resources and prevailing social stigmas. Here, mentorship can play a transformative role by offering a supportive platform for open dialogue and guidance on these critical but frequently overlooked issues.

Mentors, through relationships built on trust and mutual respect, can encourage young individuals to prioritize their health, providing them with the knowledge and resources needed to make informed health decisions. This guidance is particularly impactful in areas where there is a significant stigma attached to certain health issues, such as mental health or sexual well-being. By addressing these topics openly, mentors help destigmatize them, fostering a more supportive environment for discussing and managing health challenges.

Furthermore, mentorship can promote a holistic approach to health, emphasizing the importance of a balanced lifestyle that supports both physical and mental well-being. This can include guidance on nutrition, exercise, stress management techniques, and even time management to balance work and relaxation, all crucial for long-term health.

The role of mentorship in promoting health and well-being among Africa's youth is therefore multifaceted. It not only supports them in overcoming personal health challenges but also equips them to contribute positively to their communities. By ensuring that young people are healthy and well, mentorship helps unlock their full potential, allowing them to pursue their aspirations and lead fulfilling lives.

As we look to the future, the integration of health and well-being into mentorship programs will be key to nurturing a generation that is not only professionally successful but also healthy and well-rounded. This approach will ultimately contribute to the broader goal of developing a resilient, vibrant, and productive society across Africa.

Addressing Physical Health Challenges

In the vibrant and diverse societies of our continent, the youth stand as beacons of potential and progress. However, their ability to fully engage and drive development often hinges on their physical health, which is unfortunately impeded by a range of challenges from inadequate healthcare infrastructure to limited health education. Mentorship offers a robust solution to these challenges, enhancing both the personal well-being and collective health of young Africans.

Mentorship provides an effective platform for health education, where mentors can impart critical knowledge about maintaining a balanced diet, the benefits of regular physical exercise, and adopting healthy lifestyle choices. This guidance is crucial in regions where access to diverse food options may be limited and where daily routines may not naturally include physical activity. Mentors can offer practical advice on how to integrate nutritious foods into daily diets and incorporate physical activities into regular routines, highlighting their importance in preventing chronic diseases and improving mental health.

Moreover, navigating the complexities of healthcare systems can be daunting for many young Africans, especially those in rural or underserved areas. Mentors can play a vital role in helping them understand their rights to healthcare, the availability of services, and how to access these services effectively. This includes guidance on how to engage with healthcare providers, understanding the importance of preventive care, and navigating the often-complex pathways to receiving medical attention.

Mentors also help demystify and destigmatize conversations around health, particularly in contexts where certain topics may be considered taboo. By fostering open discussions and providing reliable information, they build trust and encourage young people to take proactive steps towards managing their health.

The broader impact of such mentorship extends beyond individual health. By promoting health literacy and proactive health management, mentors help cultivate a generation that is not only healthier but also more prepared to take on personal and professional challenges. This holistic approach not only prepares individuals to achieve their potential but also ensures a healthier future for the entire community.

In conclusion, mentorship in health is a crucial investment in the future of Africa's youth. It equips them with the knowledge, skills, and resources necessary to overcome health challenges, enabling them to lead full, active lives. This support is essential for them to harness their full potential and drive the continent's development forward, making mentorship a cornerstone not just for individual growth but for the collective advancement of society.

Supporting Mental Health And Emotional Well-Being

Supporting the mental health and emotional well-being of Africa's youth is essential for their holistic development, enabling them to tackle life's challenges with resilience and optimism. Yet, navigating the journey toward mental wellness is complex, particularly due to the pervasive stigma surrounding mental health issues in many African communities. This stigma can silence necessary conversations, discourage individuals from seeking help, and perpetuate misconceptions about mental health. In this context, mentorship emerges as a vital tool, offering support, guidance, advocacy, and a safe space for open discussion about mental and emotional well-being.

The stigma associated with mental health issues in Africa is often deeply rooted in cultural beliefs and societal norms that misinterpret or marginalize mental illness. This environment can make it difficult for young people to express their struggles or seek assistance. Mentors, through their supportive relationships with mentees, can play a transformative role in challenging these stigmas. By openly discussing mental health, sharing personal experiences, and providing accurate information, mentors help demystify mental health issues, encouraging a more compassionate and understanding perspective within communities.

Creating a safe and non-judgmental space for mentees to discuss their feelings and challenges is one of the most significant contributions mentors can make. This openness not only helps normalize conversations around mental health but also provides mentees with the reassurance that their struggles are valid, and that support is available. Such interactions can significantly impact mentees' willingness to seek professional help when needed, fostering a culture of mental health awareness and acceptance.

Another critical aspect of mentorship in supporting mental and emotional well-being is the emphasis on building resilience. Resilience—the ability to bounce back from adversity—is an invaluable skill in coping with the stressors and challenges of life. Mentors can introduce mentees to strategies and practices that bolster emotional resilience, including mindfulness, stress management techniques, and healthy coping mechanisms.

Mentors can guide mentees in setting realistic goals, managing expectations, and developing problem-solving skills that enhance their ability to deal with setbacks and challenges. By sharing stories of resilience—both their own and those of others—mentors can inspire mentees to view obstacles as opportunities for growth and learning.

Furthermore, mentors can play a crucial role in helping mentees cultivate a positive self-image and a strong sense of self-worth. Encouragement and positive reinforcement from a trusted mentor can significantly impact a mentee's confidence and outlook on life. This support is especially important in combating the feelings of isolation, inadequacy, and anxiety that can accompany mental health challenges.

In the realm of mental health and emotional well-being, mentorship stands as a beacon of hope and support for Africa's youth. By breaking the stigma surrounding mental health and fostering resilience, mentors can significantly impact the lives of mentees, equipping them with the tools necessary for emotional well-being. This support not only aids in the personal development of young individuals but also contributes to the creation of healthier, more supportive communities across the continent. Through mentorship, we can ensure that the mental and emotional well-being of Africa's future leaders is nurtured, paving the way for a stronger, more resilient generation.

Promoting Healthy Relationships And Support Systems

In the journey toward holistic well-being, the cultivation of healthy relationships and robust support systems is essential, especially for Africa's youth who are navigating the complexities of both personal and professional development. Mentorship programs stand out as a vital platform for not just providing individual guidance but also for nurturing these crucial networks and demonstrating positive behaviors.

The impact of mentorship extends well beyond the one-on-one relationship between mentor and mentee. It includes fostering a wider network of relationships that collectively support an individual's growth. Effective mentorship involves connecting mentees with a broader community including peers, seasoned professionals, and community leaders who can offer additional support, advice, and encouragement. These networks are foundational, providing emotional support and serving as resources for professional development and communal growth. Active engagement in these networks reinforces the multifaceted nature of well-being, which is shaped by a variety of relationships and interactions. Mentors can facilitate this by linking mentees to relevant groups and events and promoting peer support groups that encourage open sharing of experiences and challenges.

Mentors also serve as role models, with their behaviors, attitudes, and methods of coping being closely observed and often emulated by their mentees. This positions mentors to effectively demonstrate healthy behaviors and positive lifestyle choices that can significantly influence their mentees' well-being. Showing how to manage stress constructively, maintain work-life balance, and build healthy interpersonal relationships are all critical lessons that mentors can impart. Observing a mentor handle life's challenge with resilience and positivity provides a practical blueprint for mentees, helping them learn to navigate their own challenges effectively.

Furthermore, mentors can initiate important discussions about self-care, setting boundaries, and the importance of seeking help when needed. These conversations are vital in normalizing the care for mental and emotional health and empowering young people to take proactive steps toward their well-being.

Through mentorship, promoting healthy relationships and support systems becomes an integral strategy in enhancing the well-being of Africa's youth. This approach does not only support the personal growth and resilience of individual mentees but also contributes to building stronger, healthier communities across the continent. By laying down a foundation where well-being is a priority, mentorship ensures that young individuals have the support and guidance necessary to reach their fullest potential, shaping a future where the holistic health of the youth is a central concern.

Mentorship Programs Focused On Health And Well-Being

In Africa, the integration of health and well-being into mentorship programs is critical due to the significant challenges that impact the youth's health. These challenges range from inadequate healthcare infrastructure to limited awareness about health practices, often impeding young people's personal and professional growth. Mentorship programs provide essential support and education, profoundly altering young lives by promoting healthy lifestyles and well-being.

One notable example of a successful initiative is the Young Leaders for Health program, which pairs young individuals with mentors from the healthcare sector. This program educates mentees about crucial public health issues, nutrition, and mental wellness while also providing career guidance in health-related fields. The outcomes are promising, with participants becoming more knowledgeable about health and active as health advocates within their communities.

Another impactful mentorship initiative is the EmpowerHer program, specifically tailored for young women. This program addresses critical issues such as reproductive health, mental wellness, and gender-based violence, creating a supportive space for young women to discuss and learn about these crucial topics. The program reports positive outcomes such as enhanced self-esteem, healthier lifestyle choices, and increased academic engagement among its participants, showcasing the powerful impact mentorship can have on individuals' health and well-being.

For mentorship programs focused on health to be effective, they must adopt a holistic and thoughtful approach. This involves embracing a broad view of health that encompasses physical, mental, and emotional well-being. Creating a safe and open environment is essential for fostering discussions around sensitive health issues. This involves training mentors in empathetic communication and equipping them with the necessary resources to provide appropriate support or direct mentees to professional services.

Additionally, structured health education should be a core component of mentorship sessions, utilizing engaging materials appropriate for the mentees' age group. Leveraging technology can also enhance the reach and efficacy of these programs, providing access to health resources, workshops, and counseling services that may otherwise be unavailable.

Collaborating with health professionals can further enrich these programs, offering mentees expert insights through workshops and Q&A sessions. Monitoring and evaluating the health outcomes of these interventions are crucial for ensuring they meet their objectives and for making necessary adjustments based on feedback from mentees.

Overall, mentorship programs that focus on health and well-being are vital for supporting Africa's youth. They not only address immediate health challenges but also prepare young individuals for a healthier future, contributing significantly to the broader development goals of their communities and the continent.

In summarizing our discussions on the significance of integrating health and well-being into mentorship for Africa's youth, it's clear that such efforts are essential, not just beneficial. Mentorship transcends mere academic and professional guidance, touching on crucial aspects of physical, mental, and emotional health. This comprehensive approach equips young individuals not only for success in their careers and academic endeavors but also fortifies their overall health and resilience.

The journey to promote holistic well-being through mentorship is layered and complex. It involves dismantling stigmas around mental health, advocating for healthy lifestyle choices, and building robust support networks that facilitate open discussions about health challenges. The success stories and best practices discussed underscore the transformative potential of focused mentorship programs. These examples shine a light on effective strategies and serve as blueprints for future initiatives, emphasizing the need for a rounded approach that views young people in all facets of their development.

As we conclude, the imperative is clear for mentors, educators, policymakers, and community leaders: there is a profound need to prioritize and advocate for the integration of health and well-being into mentorship efforts. Such a holistic approach not only enhances the mentorship experience but also ensures that Africa's future generations possess the resilience, knowledge, and support necessary to navigate and overcome life's challenges. By doing so, mentorship can serve as a foundational pillar for nurturing not only the next generation of leaders and innovators but also individuals who are healthy, empowered, and fully capable of contributing to their communities and the wider world. This strategic focus on health and well-being within mentorship is crucial for fostering a healthier, more vibrant future for all.

OPTIMAL AGES FOR PARTICIPATION IN MENTORSHIP PROGRAMS

This chapter will not only serve as a guide for program developers and participants but also stress the importance of mentorship at various life stages, enhancing the overall impact of mentorship initiatives across Africa.

Introduction To Optimal Ages For Mentorship

Mentorship stands as a transformative force in Africa, offering pathways to empowerment, leadership, and innovation. Yet, the timing of engagement in mentorship roles—both as a mentee and mentor—plays a pivotal role in amplifying its impact. This nuanced understanding of the optimal ages for participation in mentorship initiatives is critical for harnessing the full potential of these interactions. This chapter delves into the ideal periods in life when African youth can most benefit from entering mentorship programs and when individuals possess the maturity, experience, and insight to guide others effectively as mentors. By identifying these key stages, we illuminate the synergy between life experience and mentorship efficacy, underscoring the strategic timing that can enhance personal development and catalyze societal change across the continent. The exploration here is grounded in the premise that mentorship, when aligned with the developmental milestones of mentees and the professional growth phases of mentors, can yield profound outcomes. It not only nurtures individual growth and aspiration but also sews the seeds for widespread social transformation in Africa. Through this analysis, I aim to provide a roadmap for individuals and organizations alike, highlighting how timely engagement in mentorship roles can shape trajectories, influence change, and contribute to the collective upliftment of African societies.

Best Age For African Youth To Join Mentorship Programs

Imagine being a teenager again, right on the cusp of adulthood, facing a world of decisions that will shape your future. For African youth, these formative years, particularly between the ages of 13 and 19, are a critical time. It's during this period that engaging in mentorship programs can truly make a difference, leveraging a time of significant cognitive, emotional, and social development to influence personal and professional trajectories profoundly.

Picture a young teen, grappling with the big questions about identity and their place in society. Adolescence is all about identity formation and self-discovery. It's a time when teenagers are asking themselves who they are and who they want to be. Now, imagine the impact a mentor can have. A mentor serves as a mirror, reflecting potential and opportunities that might not yet be visible to these young minds. Through conversations, shared activities, and exposure to new experiences, mentors help teenagers navigate their identity explorations. This engagement is crucial for building self-esteem and confidence, essential ingredients for success in any endeavor.

As these young minds ponder their futures, they face a myriad of decisions about education and career paths. The world is brimming with opportunities, which can be both exhilarating and overwhelming. Here, mentors' step in as navigators, offering insights into various fields, providing guidance on educational choices, and helping set realistic yet ambitious goals. Think of a mentor with a background in the tech industry, demystifying the path to becoming a software engineer. They advise on relevant courses, necessary skills, and valuable internships. This tailored guidance aligns academic efforts with career aspirations, ensuring mentees are well-prepared for the challenges and opportunities ahead.

But it's not just about academics and careers. Adolescence is also a crucial time for developing social and emotional competencies. Effective mentorship programs don't just focus on academic and career guidance; they also cultivate soft skills like empathy, resilience, communication, and leadership. These skills are fundamental for personal well-being, academic success, and professional achievement. Through mentorship, young individuals learn to manage social interactions, handle emotional challenges, resolve conflicts, and assume leadership roles confidently. In a rapidly changing world, adaptability and emotional intelligence are as crucial as technical skills, and mentors play a vital role in developing these competencies.

Starting mentorship at a young age instills the value of guidance, support, and advocacy, laying the groundwork for a culture of lifelong mentorship. Those who benefit from mentorship during their formative years are more likely to seek out mentors as they face new challenges and transitions later in life. Moreover, they are more inclined to become mentors themselves, recognizing the significant impact mentorship had on their own development. This creates a cycle of mentorship that ensures its sustainability and amplifies its impact across generations.

The teenage years, from 13 to 19, are identified as the optimal time for African youth to engage in mentorship programs. This period is not just about immediate benefits but also about setting a foundation for future success. The guidance provided during these years can shape the course of a young person's life, influencing their educational choices, career trajectory, and personal development.

The strategic engagement of African youth in mentorship programs during their teenage years is not just beneficial but essential. These programs play a pivotal role in shaping well-rounded, capable individuals ready to face the complexities of the modern world. By focusing on identity formation, academic and career guidance, and the development of social and emotional skills, mentorship emerges as a key lever for personal development and societal change, making the ages of 13 to 19 the most impactful years for such initiatives.

So, as you envision these young minds standing on the brink of their futures, consider the power of mentorship. It's a guiding light, illuminating paths that lead to confident, successful, and well-rounded individuals ready to make their mark on the world.

Best Age For Individuals To Become Mentors

Imagine someone in their 30s, standing at the crossroads of experience and aspiration, poised to offer guidance to those just beginning their journey. This age, often considered the prime of life, is a sweet spot for becoming a mentor. With a blend of professional expertise, life wisdom, and emotional maturity, individuals in this age range are exceptionally well-suited to mentor others.

By the time someone reaches their 30s, they've typically amassed a decade or more of professional experience. This period is filled with navigating industry changes, advancing in roles, and encountering both triumphs and setbacks. Such a rich professional background equips mentors with the ability to provide nuanced insights into career planning and industry trends. They can share hard-earned lessons from their own journeys, offer guidance on skill development, and open doors through their professional networks. All these elements can significantly influence a mentee's career trajectory, helping them avoid common pitfalls and seize opportunities.

Beyond the professional realm, those in their 30s and beyond have also accumulated a wealth of life experiences. They've often navigated significant milestones like starting families, buying homes, and making pivotal career decisions. These experiences broaden their perspective on life, allowing them to offer guidance that goes beyond mere career advice. They can help mentees balance personal and professional life, set long-term goals, and pursue paths that align with their values and aspirations. This holistic approach to mentorship ensures that mentees receive support that addresses their entire being, not just their professional ambitions.

Emotional intelligence is another key asset that tends to develop with age. With maturity comes enhanced empathy, patience, and the ability to navigate complex emotional landscapes. These qualities are fundamental to effective mentorship. Older mentors often have the patience to listen actively, the empathy to understand their mentees' struggles, and the emotional intelligence to offer supportive and non-judgmental guidance. This creates a trust-based relationship where mentees feel safe to express vulnerabilities and explore their potential without fear of criticism.

Moreover, reaching a level of personal and professional fulfillment often sparks a desire to give back. Individuals in their 30s and beyond frequently seek mentorship roles as a way to contribute to the development of the next generation. They want to share the knowledge and opportunities they've been fortunate to receive, driven by a sense of altruism. This desire to give back benefits both mentor and mentee, creating a dynamic where both parties grow. The mentor finds purpose and fulfillment in their role, while the mentee gains invaluable guidance and support.

Deciding to become a mentor is a significant commitment, one that involves dedicating time and energy to another person's growth. Those in their 30s and beyond are uniquely equipped for this role, bringing a perfect mix of professional expertise, life wisdom, and emotional maturity. They have the potential to shape the futures of their mentees profoundly, impacting not just individual lives but also contributing to the broader fabric of society. Through mentorship, they foster personal development, career success, and social change, underscoring the vital role mentors play in nurturing the next generation.

So, when considering the best age to take on the mantle of mentorship, think of someone in their 30s, standing ready to impart their accumulated wisdom and guide others toward a brighter future. It's a role that benefits both mentor and mentee, creating a legacy of shared knowledge and mutual growth.

Navigating The Timing Of Mentorship

Reflecting on my journey through a mentorship program, I've had the unique experience of seeing it from multiple angles—first as a mentee, then as a mentor, and finally as a staff member. The program I was part of set the entry age for mentees at 14, and individuals could become mentors starting at 26. I stepped into the role of a mentor at the age of 26, and over time, this experience has led me to contemplate the optimal timing for engaging in mentorship roles, both as a mentee and a mentor. Specifically, I've come to question whether joining a mentorship program at 13 instead of 14, and becoming a mentor at 30 instead of 26, might be more beneficial for both parties involved.

Engaging in a mentorship program at 13 rather than 14 can offer profound benefits for young individuals on the brink of adolescence. This pivotal age marks a crucial phase in a child's development, characterized by rapid emotional, social, and cognitive changes. The mentorship received at this formative stage can significantly shape their trajectory, providing them with the tools and guidance needed as they navigate the complexities of transitioning into adolescence.

Introducing mentorship at the age of 13 capitalizes on a critical window of opportunity for positive influence. At this age, children are beginning to form their identities, develop their sense of self, and understand their place in the world. A mentor can play a pivotal role in guiding them through these discoveries, offering advice, support, and a positive role model during a time when they are most impressionable. This early intervention can lay a strong foundation for personal development, instilling values, confidence, and aspirations that will benefit them throughout their teenage years and beyond.

The transition into high school is a significant milestone that often comes with new academic and social challenges. Starting mentorship at 13 prepares children for this transition, equipping them with coping strategies, study skills, and social competencies before they face the pressures and expectations of high school. This proactive approach ensures that mentees are not just reacting to challenges as they arise but are well-prepared to navigate them effectively from the outset.

Engaging with a mentor at 13 fosters adaptability and resilience, key qualities for thriving in both personal and academic endeavors. Through mentorship, young adolescents learn to view challenges as opportunities for growth, develop problem-solving skills, and build resilience against setbacks. These lessons are invaluable as they enter a stage of life filled with rapid changes and potential obstacles.

Starting the mentorship journey at 13 allows for the development of a long-term, meaningful relationship between the mentor and mentee. This extended timeframe provides ample opportunity for mentors to deeply understand their mentees' evolving needs, interests, and challenges, enabling them to offer more personalized and impactful guidance. The trust and rapport built over these formative years create a lasting bond that can continue to provide support and inspiration well into the mentee's future.

While the transition from childhood to adolescence is a journey marked by challenges and growth, engaging in mentorship at the age of 13 offers a strategic advantage. It provides early support and guidance that can significantly influence a young person's development, preparing them for the challenges ahead, fostering resilience, and building a foundation for lifelong learning and achievement. By embracing mentorship at this critical juncture, we can empower young individuals to navigate their formative years with confidence and purpose, setting the stage for a successful and fulfilling adolescence.

The journey into mentorship is one of profound significance, not just for the mentee but also for the mentor. While embarking on this path at 26 can be rewarding, stepping into the mentorship role at 30 offers a depth of perspective and maturity that can significantly enhance the mentorship experience. Drawing from my observations and experiences, mentors aged 30 and above tend to bring a level of commitment, insight, and impact that is distinctively more profound than their younger counterparts. This distinction is not merely chronological but is rooted in the depth of personal and professional growth that typically occurs in the years leading up to and around the age of 30.

By the age of 30, individuals often reach a pivotal stage in their careers where they've not only accumulated a decade or more of work experience but have also navigated the complexities of their industries. This experience is invaluable in mentorship, providing a rich reservoir of knowledge, skills, and real-world insights that mentors can draw upon to guide their mentees. The professional maturity and confidence gained by this age enable mentors to offer advice that is both practical and aspirational, helping mentees to navigate their own career paths more effectively.

The transition from the mid-twenties to 30 is marked by significant life milestones and experiences. Whether it's navigating successes and failures, building, or ending significant relationships, or experiencing shifts in personal values and goals, these experiences contribute to a deeper understanding of life's complexities. Mentors aged 30 and above are more likely to have faced and overcome challenges that have taught them resilience, adaptability, and the importance of work-life balance. These life lessons are invaluable to mentees, offering them a model of how to approach their personal and professional challenges with grace and resilience.

Empathy and patience are qualities that are deepened not just with age but with experience. By 30, many individuals have developed a greater capacity for empathy, allowing them to connect with mentees on a more profound level. They are more adept at listening, understanding, and responding to the needs and concerns of their mentees with sensitivity and insight. Additionally, the patience honed through years of personal and professional growth enables mentors to guide their mentees through their development process without rushing or imposing unrealistic expectations.

Entering mentorship at 30 often coincides with a period of increased stability in one's personal and professional life. This stability allows for a greater commitment to the mentorship process, ensuring that mentors can provide consistent, focused attention to their mentees. The commitment is not just a function of time but of the mentor's readiness to invest emotionally and intellectually in the growth and success of their mentees.

Choosing to become a mentor at 30, rather than 26, offers a unique opportunity to leverage a more mature and rounded perspective on life and career. The additional years provide mentors with a depth of experience, wisdom, and stability that enrich the mentorship experience, making it more impactful for the mentee. This is not to diminish the value that younger mentors bring to the table but to highlight the distinct advantages that come with stepping into mentorship at a later stage. As mentors aged 30 and above share their journey, they not only guide their mentees towards success but also model the richness of a life well-lived and a career thoughtfully navigated.

The exploration of optimal ages for participation in mentorship programs underscores the profound impact that timing can have on the effectiveness and transformational power of mentorship. By engaging African youth at the critical developmental window of 13 to 19 years and enlisting the mentorship of those aged 30 and above, we harness a unique combination of youthful potential and mature insight. This approach not only maximizes the benefits of mentorship for individuals but also amplifies its ripple effects across communities and societies at large

For mentees, beginning mentorship during their formative teenage years provides a foundation of support, guidance, and inspiration precisely when they are navigating the complexities of identity, academic choices, and early career considerations. This timing ensures that mentorship acts as a catalyst for growth, empowering young individuals with the tools, confidence, and vision needed to pursue their aspirations and contribute positively to society.

Conversely, mentors aged 30 and above bring to the table a depth of life and professional experiences that enrich the mentorship experience. Their insights, forged through varied challenges and achievements, provide mentees with a wealth of knowledge and perspectives that can guide them through their own journeys. The maturity, empathy, and stability that come with age enable these mentors to offer nuanced, compassionate guidance that resonates deeply with mentees, fostering meaningful relationships and impactful learning experiences.

This age-specific engagement in mentorship is not merely a matter of pairing individuals; it is about creating a symbiotic ecosystem where the growth of one directly contributes to the development of the other. It ensures that mentorship remains a powerful tool for personal development, career advancement, and societal progress, nurturing a cycle of learning, growth, and giving back that can sustain and propel the continent forward.

The strategic timing of involvement in mentorship programs is a key lever for unlocking the full potential of Africa's youth and the experienced professionals poised to guide them. As we continue to refine and advocate for these age-specific approaches to mentorship, we lay the groundwork for a future where every African youth has the opportunity to thrive, supported by the wisdom and experience of those who have navigated the path before them. This vision for mentorship not only promises to change individual lives but to reshape the societal landscape of Africa, driving sustainable development and fostering a continent rich in leadership, innovation, and community solidarity.

NAVIGATING THE HURDLES: OVERCOMING CHALLENGES IN AFRICAN MENTORSHIP PROGRAMS

In Chapter 7, the focus shifts to the hurdles faced by mentorship programs in Africa and the strategies needed to overcome them. Mentorship programs are vital for bridging gaps in education, professional development, and personal growth, preparing African youth for leadership roles in a promising future. Yet, creating and sustaining impactful mentorship initiatives is no easy feat. The challenges range from logistical issues like funding and resource allocation to more subtle barriers such as societal norms and cultural expectations.

These obstacles can have a significant impact on the success and longevity of mentorship programs. Addressing both external factors, like the digital divide and geographical disparities that limit access to mentorship, and internal challenges, including the necessity for thorough mentor training and fostering meaningful mentor-mentee connections, is essential. The chapter also delves into broader societal and cultural issues, such as gender inequality, the stigma around personal and professional development, and the underrepresentation of certain groups within mentorship programs.

Through a detailed exploration of these challenges, the chapter provides strategic insights and practical solutions for program organizers, mentors, and stakeholders. Overcoming these hurdles is crucial for enhancing the effectiveness of mentorship programs, enabling them to fully support the transformational growth of Africa's youth. The goal is to ensure that mentorship programs can thrive, adapt, and expand to meet the diverse and dynamic needs of Africa's youth, significantly contributing to the continent's overall developmental trajectory.

Recruitment And Retention Of Mentors

Recruiting and retaining mentors for mentorship programs across Africa is both an art and a science. The success and impact of these programs hinge critically on the ability and willingness of mentors to commit their time, expertise, and emotional resources to support mentees. Despite the pivotal role mentors play, attracting and keeping them presents complex challenges. These challenges often stem from time constraints, a lack of awareness about the program's value, and unclear incentives for participation. Addressing these issues is essential for building a robust mentorship program that can truly transform lives.

The primary hurdle in recruiting mentors is finding individuals who possess the right mix of expertise, experience, and a genuine desire to help others grow. Many potential mentors juggle demanding careers and personal commitments, making time a scarce commodity. Moreover, there is often a lack of awareness about the existence and benefits of mentorship programs. Even when individuals are aware, they might not see the immediate personal or professional benefits of participating, especially if they perceive mentorship as a one-sided affair that demands their input without offering anything in return.

Another challenge lies in aligning mentors' skills and experiences with the specific needs of mentees. Many mentorship programs cater to youths facing diverse challenges or aspiring to various career paths, necessitating a broad spectrum of mentors. This diversity requirement can complicate the recruitment process, as programs must not only find willing participants but also those whose backgrounds and expertise match the mentees' needs.

To overcome these challenges, mentorship programs must adopt strategic approaches to recruitment. Highlighting the personal and professional benefits of mentoring can shift potential mentors' perception of participation. Emphasizing that mentorship is a two-way street, offering mentors personal growth, expanded networks, and the fulfillment that comes from making a tangible difference in someone's life, can make the role more appealing.

Providing comprehensive training and support for mentors can also alleviate concerns about time and commitment. By offering resources that help mentors engage effectively with their mentees, programs can assure potential volunteers that they won't be navigating the mentorship journey alone. Additionally, leveraging community leaders and professionals who are already seen as role models can encourage others to participate. Their involvement can lend credibility to the program and inspire others to contribute.

While financial incentives may not be feasible or desirable for all mentorship programs, other forms of recognition and rewards can play a crucial role in attracting and retaining mentors. Certificates of recognition, awards, and public acknowledgment of mentors' contributions can provide tangible tokens of appreciation that underscore the value of their volunteerism.

Moreover, offering professional development opportunities—such as workshops, seminars, and networking events exclusively for mentors—can enhance the appeal of joining a mentorship program. These opportunities not only benefit mentors professionally but also create a sense of community among them, fostering a network of individuals committed to personal and societal growth.

Creating a supportive, engaged community of mentors can itself become an incentive. When mentors feel part of a collective endeavor, supported by their peers and the program organizers, their commitment to mentorship is likely to deepen. Providing platforms for mentors to share experiences, challenges, and successes can reinforce the communal aspect of mentorship, making retention more likely.

Recruiting and retaining mentors for African mentorship programs requires a nuanced understanding of the challenges and an innovative approach to addressing them. By highlighting the mutual benefits of mentorship, providing robust support, and training, and recognizing mentors' contributions, programs can attract the dedicated individuals needed to make a meaningful impact. These strategies, coupled with the creation of a supportive mentor community, lay the foundation for a sustainable mentorship program that can continue to enrich the lives of Africa's youth and contribute to the continent's broader development goals.

Building such a program takes time and effort, but the rewards are immense. When mentors see the impact of their guidance, support and advocacy on young lives, the sense of fulfillment and purpose is profound. This not only benefits the mentees but also enhances the mentors' own personal and professional growth. It creates a ripple effect, where the benefits of mentorship extend beyond the immediate relationships and contribute to a culture of giving and growth within the community.

In conclusion, effective mentor recruitment and retention are crucial for the success of mentorship programs. By addressing the challenges head-on and implementing thoughtful strategies, we can create robust programs that support the transformational growth of Africa's youth. This ensures that the next generation is equipped with the guidance, support, and opportunities they need to thrive and lead, ultimately contributing to the continent's broader developmental trajectory.

Funding And Resource Allocation

Mentorship programs, so crucial in shaping the futures of young Africans, often face the daunting challenge of securing and managing funding. This financial aspect is critical, affecting every facet of program operations—from inception and execution to expansion and sustainability. Understanding these financial hurdles and exploring diversified solutions for financial stability are essential steps toward ensuring the success and longevity of mentorship initiatives.

The financial landscape for mentorship programs is fraught with challenges. Initial funding, crucial for kick-starting programs, often poses the first significant hurdle. Many programs rely on external funding sources, which can be highly competitive and subject to the changing priorities of donors. Beyond the initial setup, securing consistent funding to cover operational costs, such as training materials, administrative support, and program activities, presents an ongoing challenge.

Ensuring long-term sustainability is perhaps the most significant financial challenge. As programs grow, so do their financial needs. Expanding services to reach more mentees, enhancing program offerings, and maintaining the quality of mentorship all require additional resources. Without a stable financial base, even the most impactful programs risk reduction in services or, worse, closure.

Achieving financial stability necessitates a multifaceted approach, incorporating various funding models and innovative fundraising strategies. Partnerships with the private sector can unlock corporate social responsibility (CSR) funds, while grants from international organizations and governments offer substantial support for development-focused initiatives. These partnerships not only provide financial backing but can also lend credibility and visibility to mentorship programs, attracting further support.

Community-based fundraising efforts tap into the local support base, engaging those who directly benefit from or support the program's goals. These efforts can range from small-scale local events to larger campaigns, fostering a sense of ownership and investment within the community.

Diversifying funding sources is crucial for financial resilience. Grants from foundations and international bodies, though competitive, can offer significant support. Engaging the private sector through corporate sponsorships provides an avenue for businesses to contribute to their communities' development, aligning with their CSR objectives.

Public-private partnerships represent another strategy, combining government support with private sector efficiency and resources. This collaborative approach can leverage the strengths of both sectors to achieve mutual development goals.

Crowdfunding and social entrepreneurship present innovative funding models that capitalize on the power of collective support and the generation of revenue through social ventures, respectively. These approaches can mobilize broader community support and create sustainable income streams to support mentorship activities.

Effective budget management and transparency are foundational to building and maintaining trust with donors, partners, and the communities served. Clear financial planning, regular reporting, and open communication about how funds are used reassure stakeholders of the program's integrity and commitment to its mission. This transparency not only aids in retaining current supporters but can also attract new donors who are assured of the program's accountability and effective use of resources.

Implementing strict financial controls, conducting regular audits, and publishing annual reports are practices that enhance transparency. Furthermore, engaging stakeholders in discussions about financial needs and program outcomes can foster a sense of collaboration and mutual investment in the program's success.

Navigating the financial challenges of running mentorship programs requires creativity, strategic planning, and a commitment to transparency. By diversifying funding streams, forging strategic partnerships, and implementing efficient budget management, mentorship programs can lay a solid foundation for financial stability. This stability ensures that mentorship initiatives can continue to make a profound impact on the lives of Africa's youth, guiding them toward brighter futures while contributing to the continent's overall development.

In the end, the resilience and growth of mentorship programs hinge on their ability to secure and effectively allocate resources, making financial strategy a cornerstone of successful mentorship initiatives. By adopting a comprehensive approach to funding and resource allocation, mentorship programs can sustain their efforts, expand their reach, and deepen their impact, ultimately helping to foster a generation of empowered, capable, and visionary African youth ready to lead and innovate in their communities and beyond.

Cultural And Societal Barriers

In the rich tapestry of African societies, cultural and societal norms play a pivotal role in shaping interactions and relationships. While these norms can foster a sense of community and belonging, they may also pose significant barriers to the implementation and effectiveness of mentorship programs. Understanding and navigating these cultural and societal barriers is crucial for the success of mentorship initiatives aimed at empowering the continent's youth.

One of the primary cultural barriers to mentorship in Africa is the traditional hierarchy and respect for authority. In many African cultures, there exists a deeply ingrained respect for elders and those in authority positions. This respect can sometimes create a gap between potential mentors and mentees. Young people may feel hesitant to engage openly in a mentorship relationship with an elder or someone they perceive as being in a position of authority, fearing that it may be seen as disrespectful or that their questions may be unwelcome.

Additionally, cultural perceptions of mentorship itself can vary widely. In some communities, the concept of mentorship—as understood in a more Western context—may be unfamiliar or perceived as unnecessary. Informal guidance from family members or community elders is often seen as sufficient. This can make the formal establishment of mentorship programs challenging, as the perceived value may not be immediately recognized.

To effectively implement mentorship programs in such diverse cultural landscapes, it's essential to work within these cultural contexts to promote the value of mentorship. This requires a multi-faceted approach, combining community engagement, education, and advocacy to shift perceptions and highlight the benefits of mentorship for individual and communal growth.

Community engagement is crucial. Initiatives that seek to introduce mentorship programs must first invest time in understanding the specific cultural dynamics of the communities they wish to serve. Engagement efforts can include discussions with community leaders, elders, and potential mentees to gather insights and garner support. By involving the community in the conversation from the outset, programs can tailor their approaches to be more culturally sensitive and relevant.

Education and advocacy play vital roles in changing societal perceptions of mentorship. This can involve creating awareness about the benefits of mentorship beyond the informal guidance traditionally offered within communities. Highlighting success stories and outcomes from mentorship programs—such as improved academic performance, career advancements, or personal growth—can help demonstrate the tangible value of formal mentorship.

Strategies for promoting mentorship within cultural contexts also include showcasing how mentorship can complement, rather than replace, traditional forms of guidance. Emphasizing that mentorship programs aim to build upon the existing foundations of community support and wisdom can help alleviate concerns about mentorship undermining cultural norms or hierarchies.

Moreover, advocacy efforts can focus on the broader benefits of mentorship for societal development, such as fostering innovation, leadership, and social cohesion. By presenting mentorship as a tool for communal advancement, programs can appeal to the collective values of African societies, encouraging a more receptive attitude towards mentorship initiatives.

Cultural and societal barriers present significant challenges to the implementation and effectiveness of mentorship programs in Africa. However, by carefully navigating cultural norms, engaging with communities, and employing strategic education and advocacy, these barriers can be overcome. Successful mentorship programs are those that respect and incorporate cultural values, work to shift perceptions of mentorship, and demonstrate the concrete benefits of such initiatives for individuals and communities alike. In doing so, mentorship can become a valued and integral part of African societies, contributing to the empowerment of the continent's youth and the broader goal of sustainable development.

Navigating these barriers requires patience, sensitivity, and a genuine commitment to understanding the communities served. By building trust and showing respect for cultural traditions, mentorship programs can create an environment where young people feel supported and encouraged to grow. The journey may be challenging, but the potential rewards—in terms of personal development, community strength, and societal progress—make it a worthy endeavor.

Ensuring Program Quality And Impact

Ensuring the quality and impact of mentorship programs is essential for their success and sustainability. However, the path to achieving and demonstrating significant outcomes is fraught with challenges. These include difficulties in measuring impact, setting clear objectives, and implementing quality assurance strategies. Addressing these issues head-on is crucial for mentorship programs to fulfill their mission of transforming lives and contributing to broader societal development.

One of the primary hurdles mentorship programs face is quantifying and demonstrating their impact. The transformative effects of mentorship—such as increased self-confidence, improved academic performance, or enhanced professional skills—can be profound yet challenging to measure with traditional metrics. Furthermore, the long-term nature of many benefits makes immediate assessment difficult, complicating efforts to attribute specific outcomes directly to the program.

Another challenge lies in the diversity of mentorship goals and participant backgrounds, which can result in a wide array of outcomes, not all of which are easily quantifiable. This variability requires a nuanced approach to impact assessment that can accommodate the multifaceted nature of mentorship benefits.

To overcome these challenges and ensure both quality and impact, mentorship programs must adopt robust quality assurance strategies. These strategies should be comprehensive, encompassing clear goal setting, meticulous data collection, and the integration of feedback into program design.

The foundation of any effective mentorship program is clear, measurable objectives. These goals should be aligned with the needs of the mentees and the broader aims of the program, whether focusing on academic achievement, career development, personal growth, or a combination of these areas. Objectives should be Specific, Measurable, Achievable, Relevant, and Time-bound (SMART), providing a framework for assessing progress and impact.

Data collection is vital for tracking progress toward objectives and evaluating the program's effectiveness. This process should include both quantitative and qualitative data to capture the full spectrum of mentorship outcomes. Quantitative measures might include academic scores, employment rates, or participation levels, while qualitative data can be gathered through surveys, interviews, and case studies that reflect mentees' experiences and perceptions.

Innovative tools and technologies can facilitate data collection, enabling real-time tracking and analysis. However, it's crucial to ensure that data collection methods are ethical, respect privacy, and are sensitive to the cultural context of participants.

Feedback from mentees, mentors, and other stakeholders is an invaluable resource for program improvement. This feedback can identify areas of strength and highlight aspects of the program that may require refinement. Regular review meetings, feedback surveys, and open forums for discussion can foster a culture of continuous improvement, ensuring that the program remains responsive to participants' needs and adapts to changing contexts.

Incorporating feedback effectively requires an organizational commitment to learning and adaptability. It may involve revising training materials for mentors, altering program activities to better meet mentees' needs, or even rethinking program objectives based on emerging insights.

Ensuring the quality and impact of mentorship programs is a complex but essential task. By setting clear objectives, employing rigorous data collection methods, and integrating feedback into program design, mentorship initiatives can navigate the challenges of impact measurement. These strategies not only facilitate the demonstration of tangible outcomes but also contribute to the continuous improvement of program quality.

Ultimately, the success of mentorship programs in transforming the lives of Africa's youth and achieving broader developmental goals hinges on their ability to prove and enhance their effectiveness over time. Through dedicated effort and strategic planning, mentorship programs can leave a lasting imprint on individuals and communities alike, marking a path toward a brighter, more empowered future.

It's the kind of effort that requires everyone involved to be fully committed to the process. Mentors and mentees alike need to see the value in their participation and feel that their contributions are recognized and impactful. When everyone is engaged, the quality and impact of the program naturally improve. The real beauty of mentorship lies in its ability to evolve, adapt, and respond to the needs of those it serves. By embracing this dynamic nature, mentorship programs can truly become catalysts for positive change, shaping the next generation of leaders and innovators in Africa.

Leveraging Technology For Mentorship

In an era where technology profoundly impacts education, communication, and social interaction, leveraging digital solutions for mentorship programs can significantly enhance their reach and effectiveness. However, integrating technology into mentorship initiatives, particularly in regions with limited access to digital infrastructure, poses distinct challenges. Despite these obstacles, the potential benefits of embracing digital solutions for mentorship are immense, offering innovative ways to connect mentors and mentees, provide training, and facilitate meaningful interactions.

The primary challenge in leveraging technology for mentorship in Africa is the digital divide—the gap between those with easy access to digital technology and the internet and those without. In many parts of the continent, especially in rural and underserved areas, limited internet connectivity, the high cost of data, and a lack of digital devices restrict access to online platforms. Furthermore, variations in digital literacy levels among potential mentors and mentees can hinder the effective use of technology-based solutions.

Another challenge is ensuring the privacy and security of online interactions. As mentorship programs move to digital platforms, protecting sensitive information and maintaining the confidentiality of mentor-mentee communications become paramount concerns that must be addressed through robust cybersecurity measures.

Despite these barriers, the potential of technology to transform mentorship programs is undeniable. Here are several ways to incorporate technology into mentorship initiatives:

Digital platforms can streamline the process of training mentors and matching them with mentees. E-learning modules can provide mentors with the necessary skills and knowledge for effective mentoring, regardless of their location. Similarly, sophisticated algorithms can facilitate the matching process, ensuring that mentors and mentees with complementary needs, interests, and backgrounds are paired, enhancing the likelihood of a successful mentorship relationship.

Technology enables continuous and flexible communication between mentors and mentees. Messaging apps, video calls, and online forums can provide various channels for interaction, making it easier for mentors and mentees to stay in touch, share resources, and hold regular mentoring sessions, even across great distances.

Online libraries, educational websites, and other digital resources can greatly enrich the mentorship experience. Mentors can guide mentees to relevant online courses, webinars, and literature, facilitating their learning and professional development.

To overcome the challenges of limited digital access, mentorship programs can employ a blended approach, combining face-to-face interactions with digital communication where possible. For areas with minimal internet connectivity, leveraging SMS-based mentoring or utilizing radio and television broadcasts for educational content can be effective alternatives.

Integrating digital literacy training into mentorship programs can empower both mentors and mentees to make the most of available technology. This training can cover basic computer skills, internet safety, and the effective use of digital tools for learning and communication.

Leveraging technology for mentorship offers a pathway to overcoming geographical barriers, enhancing the quality of mentorship provided, and ensuring that more young people can benefit from these programs. While challenges exist, particularly in regions with limited digital access, innovative solutions and a commitment to inclusivity can enable mentorship programs to harness the power of technology effectively. By embracing digital solutions, mentorship initiatives can expand their reach, offering transformative experiences to mentors and mentees alike and contributing significantly to personal and professional development across the continent.

Incorporating technology into mentorship isn't just about adapting to modern trends; it's about expanding possibilities and making mentorship accessible to everyone, regardless of their location. The potential for online platforms to democratize access to resources and support is immense. With careful planning and a focus on overcoming barriers, technology can be a powerful ally in creating impactful mentorship programs that shape the future of Africa's youth. This journey requires resilience, creativity, and a willingness to innovate, but the rewards—empowered, connected, and capable young people—are well worth the effort.

Sustainable Strategies And Solutions

Sustainable strategies and solutions are the bedrock upon which mentorship programs can build a lasting legacy. In the dynamic landscapes of African societies, where economic, social, and technological environments are constantly evolving, the sustainability of mentorship programs becomes paramount. This sustainability ensures that programs can continue to make a profound impact, adapting to meet the changing needs of the youth they serve.

The foundation of sustainable mentorship programs lies in the engagement and support of the local community. When communities are involved in the development and operation of mentorship initiatives, they gain a sense of ownership and investment in the program's success. This engagement can take various forms, from involving community leaders in program planning to recruiting local mentors who understand the cultural and societal context of their mentees.

Community support also opens avenues for sustainable volunteer and financial backing. By illustrating the tangible benefits of mentorship, such as improved educational outcomes, enhanced employability, and personal development among participants, programs can galvanize community members to contribute, whether through volunteering, donations, or other forms of support. This grassroots level of involvement ensures the program's relevance and adaptability to the community's needs, fostering a sustainable model of operation.

Flexibility and adaptability are key characteristics of sustainable mentorship programs. As societal needs, technological capabilities, and economic conditions change, so too must mentorship initiatives evolve to remain effective. This evolution can involve incorporating new technological tools to facilitate mentor-mentee communication, updating program content to reflect current realities, or expanding program objectives to address emerging challenges faced by the youth.

Leveraging digital platforms for mentorship is one way to enhance the program's reach and efficiency. Online mentoring can overcome geographical barriers, connecting mentors and mentees across vast distances and making the program accessible to a broader audience. However, this digital approach should complement, not replace, the personal connections that form the heart of mentorship, ensuring that the program maintains its impact in a changing world.

The success of mentorship programs largely depends on the quality and dedication of the mentors themselves. Providing continuous training and support is crucial in ensuring mentors are well-equipped to guide their mentees effectively. This support can include initial training sessions that cover the basics of mentorship, communication skills, and cultural sensitivity, as well as ongoing opportunities for professional development.

Creating a supportive community among mentors is equally important. Peer support networks, mentor meetups, and online forums can offer mentors a platform to share experiences, challenges, and successes. This sense of community not only aids in navigating the intricacies of mentorship but also enhances mentor retention by fostering a collaborative and supportive environment.

Furthermore, recognizing and rewarding the contributions of mentors can reinforce their commitment to the program.

Acknowledgment can come in many forms, from formal awards and recognition events to simple expressions of gratitude from mentees and program organizers. These gestures of appreciation highlight the value of mentors' contributions, encouraging their continued involvement and attracting new volunteers to the program.

Sustainable strategies and solutions are essential for mentorship programs aiming to make a lasting impact on the lives of Africa's youth. By building strong community support, remaining adaptable to change, and providing comprehensive training and support for mentors, these programs can ensure their continued relevance and effectiveness. As mentorship initiatives navigate the complexities of creating sustainable change, their efforts can lay the groundwork for a future where every young African has the guidance, support, and opportunities needed to thrive. Through sustained commitment and strategic planning, mentorship programs can contribute significantly to the personal development of mentees and the broader socio-economic development of the continent.

It's a journey that requires dedication and strategic planning, but the rewards are immense. By fostering a culture of support and adaptability, mentorship programs can create lasting change and empower the next generation of African leaders. This commitment to sustainability not only ensures the longevity of these programs but also enhances their ability to make a profound and lasting difference in the lives of countless young people.

As we draw this chapter to a close, it's clear that the pathway to establishing successful and enduring mentorship programs in Africa is fraught with challenges. Yet, through resilience, innovation, and a deep commitment to community engagement, these obstacles can not only be navigated but transformed into opportunities for growth and enhancement. This chapter has underscored the importance of a collaborative approach, rallying mentors, mentees, community leaders, and organizations towards a common goal: to forge mentorship initiatives that are not just impactful in the short term but sustainable over the long haul.

The essence of overcoming these hurdles lies in recognizing the dynamic nature of mentorship programs and the environments in which they operate. By fostering a sense of ownership within local communities, programs can ensure relevance and responsiveness to the needs at hand. Similarly, embracing adaptability—whether through the integration of technology, the fine-tuning of mentor training, or the anticipation of societal shifts—ensures that mentorship remains effective and meaningful in a rapidly changing world.

Ultimately, the journey of mentorship programs in Africa is one of collective effort and shared vision. It is a call to action for stakeholders at all levels to contribute their part in nurturing environments where mentorship can flourish. By doing so, we pave the way for mentorship to be a powerful catalyst for personal growth, professional development, and broader social change across the continent. This shared commitment and collaborative spirit are what will drive the continued success and evolution of mentorship programs, making a lasting impact on the lives of Africa's youth.

THE ROLE OF GOVERNMENT AND THE AFRICAN UNION IN MENTORSHIP

The role of governmental bodies and the African Union (AU) in the landscape of mentorship across Africa is pivotal. These entities possess unique capabilities to structurally support, legitimate, and resource mentorship initiatives, effectively bridging the gap between individual efforts and broader national and continental developmental objectives.

The involvement of government and the AU goes beyond mere endorsement. It involves active participation in crafting ecosystems that foster growth, innovation, and inclusivity. Through comprehensive policy frameworks, governments and the AU can establish standards and provide guidance that ensures mentorship programs are well-aligned with wider educational, economic, and social goals. This support is crucial in providing the necessary resources—financial, technological, and human—that enable mentorship initiatives to thrive and expand.

This chapter explores the intricate relationship between these governmental bodies, the AU, and mentorship programs. It highlights successful examples where collaboration between these entities and mentorship initiatives has significantly impacted youth empowerment and professional development, contributing positively to societal advancement. These case studies illustrate the mechanisms through which support from governments and the AU can enhance the effectiveness of mentorship programs, which in turn supports the stability and development of African societies.

The active engagement of these bodies underscores their acknowledgment of mentorship's critical role not only in individual growth but also as a foundational element of societal progress. The discussion in this chapter sheds light on how the involvement of government and the AU can catalyze transformative change, creating environments where every young African has the opportunity to reach their full potential. The vision presented is one of a continent where mentorship is deeply integrated into the fabric of development, supported, and sustained by the concerted efforts of national and continental governance structures.

By actively supporting mentorship, these bodies ensure that programs are not just effective but sustainable, helping to cultivate a generation of empowered leaders ready to drive Africa's future. Through policies, resources, and an unwavering commitment to youth development, governments and the AU can create a robust foundation for mentorship that permeates every level of society, fostering a culture of continuous learning and growth.

Policy Frameworks And Support

The active engagement of governments and the African Union (AU) in crafting supportive policy frameworks is crucial for the successful implementation and sustainability of mentorship programs across Africa. These policies not only facilitate the establishment of mentorship initiatives but also ensure their effectiveness and alignment with broader developmental goals.

Governments and the AU can play a transformative role by establishing comprehensive national standards for mentorship. Such standards would define the core principles, ethical guidelines, and best practices for mentorship programs, ensuring consistency and quality across various initiatives. By setting these standards, these bodies not only enhance the structural integrity of mentorship programs but also bolster public and stakeholder trust in their efficacy and value. Developing these standards would involve a collaborative effort, incorporating insights from educators, mentorship experts, and community leaders to address diverse needs and regional differences effectively.

Beyond policy creation, the provision of financial and logistical support is vital. Government and AU funding can significantly alleviate the resource constraints many mentorships' programs face, covering essential aspects like training, materials, and the coordination of mentor-mentee engagements. Such support is not merely a financial commitment but a reflection of a strategic investment in the continent's future leadership and workforce.

Governments and the AU can further aid mentorship programs by providing access to necessary facilities and technological resources. This can include offering spaces for meetings and workshops or investing in digital platforms that facilitate remote mentoring, crucial in reaching a wider audience and overcoming geographical barriers. By enhancing accessibility, these bodies ensure that mentorship benefits are extended to a broader segment of the youth population, including those in underserved or remote areas.

Embedding mentorship initiatives within larger educational and youth development strategies can magnify their impact. This alignment ensures that mentorship programs contribute directly to national development goals, such as improving educational outcomes, reducing youth unemployment, and fostering social cohesion.

The role of governmental and continental bodies like the AU in supporting mentorship programs through thoughtful policy frameworks, adequate funding, and logistical backing is indispensable. Such support not only solidifies the foundation of these programs but also enhances their capacity to foster a generation that is well-equipped to navigate the complexities of the modern world and lead Africa towards sustainable growth and development. Through these concerted efforts, mentorship can become a cornerstone of Africa's strategy to cultivate a resilient, skilled, and innovative youth population.

It's through these deliberate and structured approaches that governments and the AU can ensure mentorship programs are not just temporary initiatives but enduring pillars of youth development. This sustained effort will help create a future where African youth are empowered, capable, and ready to contribute meaningfully to their communities and beyond. By investing in mentorship, we invest in the very fabric of our societies, fostering a legacy of continuous growth and improvement.

Case Studies Of Government-Backed Initiatives

The effectiveness of government and African Union (AU)-backed mentorship initiatives across Africa can be compellingly demonstrated through specific case studies, each highlighting how structured support can facilitate significant improvements in youth development and societal progress.

One standout example is the AU Youth Volunteer Corps. This program encapsulates the spirit of pan-African cooperation, designed to mobilize the continent's youth toward leadership and community service across diverse sectors such as education, health, and peacebuilding. The mentorship component of the program is vital; it pairs young volunteers with seasoned professionals in their fields of deployment, enhancing skill transfer and fostering a sense of pan-African identity and dedication to the continent's development goals. This program not only equips the youth with necessary skills and experiences but also instills in them a commitment to contributing positively to societal challenges and opportunities across Africa.

In Rwanda, the government's integration of mentorship into national strategies for youth development showcases another effective approach. Rwanda has launched various initiatives aimed at building leadership qualities and entrepreneurial skills among its young population. The Imbuto Foundation, for instance, connects young Rwandans with mentors from diverse professional backgrounds, emphasizing leadership, career development, and personal growth. This mentorship is instrumental in boosting the confidence and capabilities of participants, enabling them to pursue their aspirations more effectively. Additionally, Rwanda has incorporated mentorship programs into its educational system, aiming to complement traditional academic education with practical experience and life skills focused on leadership and entrepreneurship.

These initiatives have led to tangible outcomes, including the development of young entrepreneurs and community leaders who credit their success to the support and guidance received through these mentorship programs. Rwanda's model illustrates how national mentorship programs can not only support individual youth development but also contribute to wider national development goals.

These case studies—the AU Youth Volunteer Corps and Rwanda's national mentorship initiatives—serve as robust examples of how governmental and AU support can significantly enhance the scope and impact of mentorship programs. They underscore the potential of these programs to mold a generation of well-prepared leaders who are capable of driving positive change across the continent.

Through continued commitment and strategic collaboration between governments, the AU, and other key stakeholders, such initiatives can maintain their critical role in empowering African youth and advancing the developmental agenda of the continent. These efforts highlight the transformative potential of mentorship when aligned with structured support and comprehensive developmental strategies.

Benefits To Societal Development And Stability

Mentorship programs, especially those supported by governments and the African Union (AU), play a pivotal role in the broader spectrum of societal development and stability across Africa. These programs do more than just provide personal and professional growth; they empower young Africans to actively engage in and contribute to their communities and economies.

Central to the benefits of these programs is the empowerment of the continent's youth. Access to experienced mentors who provide insights into various careers, along with leadership and personal development, equips young people with essential skills, confidence, and resilience. This empowerment is critical for fostering economic growth and innovation, enabling the youth to spearhead startups, innovate new products and services, and contribute to economic diversity and dynamism. A confident, skilled young workforce is indispensable for propelling economic advancements and ensuring the sustainability of growth across diverse sectors.

Mentorship also fosters social cohesion and unity. By bridging diverse groups—bringing together individuals from different backgrounds, ethnicities, and regions—these programs enhance understanding and collaboration within diverse populations. Such initiatives are particularly potent in nations where ethnic tensions or social fragmentation prevail, as they can forge unity and peace, building a foundation for a more cohesive society.

Mentorship directly addresses one of Africa's most pressing challenges: youth unemployment. Programs that provide career guidance, enhance professional skills, and facilitate networking pave the way for young individuals to successfully enter the job market. Emphasizing entrepreneurship within these programs encourages young people to start their own businesses, which in turn stimulates job creation and economic diversification.

Focusing mentorship on key developmental sectors like agriculture, technology, and renewable energy ensures that the upcoming workforce is not only employable but also primed to lead and innovate within these critical industries. Aligning mentorship efforts with national development goals enhances young people's employability and ensures that the workforce can meet future economic needs.

The backing of mentorship initiatives by governments and the AU represents a strategic investment in Africa's future, vital for societal development and stability. These efforts foster a prosperous, cohesive, and stable environment where the youth can thrive. The success of these initiatives is thus integral not only to individual success but also to the societal well-being and progress of the continent. With sustained support and expansion, these mentorship programs have the potential to significantly shape Africa's future, ensuring it is marked by increased resilience and prosperity.

Ultimately, the success of mentorship programs extends beyond personal achievements. They are a cornerstone for building a society where the youth are empowered, economies are robust, and communities are united. These programs are not just an investment in individuals, but in the collective future of Africa, fostering a landscape where growth, innovation, and stability can flourish.

Why Government Should Support Mentorship Programs

The support of mentorship programs by governments and the African Union (AU) is not merely a policy choice; it is a strategic investment in the future of the continent. This support is vital for nurturing the potential of Africa's youth, ensuring their contributions to national and continental development are maximized. The rationale for such support is multifaceted, encompassing the development of human capital, the fostering of innovation and entrepreneurship, and the achievement of Sustainable Development Goals (SDGs).

At the core of the argument for governmental and AU support of mentorship programs is the concept of human capital development. Human capital—the knowledge, skills, and health that people accumulate over their lives—is a critical driver of sustainable development and economic competitiveness. Mentorship programs play a crucial role in this regard, offering young individuals personalized guidance, skill enhancement, and professional development opportunities. By investing in mentorship, governments and the AU are directly investing in the enhancement of their populations' capabilities and productivity, which is essential for fostering economic growth and societal well-being.

Mentorship programs serve as incubators for innovation and entrepreneurship, nurturing the creative potential of the youth and guiding them toward realizing their entrepreneurial ambitions. In a continent as diverse and resource-rich as Africa, innovation and entrepreneurship are key to solving longstanding challenges and driving economic diversification and resilience. Through mentorship, young entrepreneurs gain access to valuable insights, networks, and support systems that can help them navigate the complexities of starting and scaling businesses. Governmental and AU support for such programs not only catalyzes the creation of new enterprises but also contributes to building an ecosystem that sustains innovation and entrepreneurship.

Furthermore, mentorship initiatives directly contribute to the achievement of several Sustainable Development Goals (SDGs). These global goals, adopted by all United Nations Member States, include quality education (SDG 4), gender equality (SDG 5), decent work and economic growth (SDG 8), and reduced inequalities (SDG 10). Mentorship programs, by providing education and skill-building opportunities, supporting the empowerment of women and underrepresented groups, and fostering job creation and economic activity, are aligned with the ethos of the SDGs. Governmental and AU support for mentorship is, therefore, an investment in the progress toward these global objectives, demonstrating a commitment to sustainable development and international cooperation.

The support of mentorship programs by governments and the African Union is imperative for the holistic development of Africa's youth and the broader societal advancement. Such support not only enhances the continent's human capital and fosters innovation and entrepreneurship but also aligns with the commitment to achieving the Sustainable Development Goals. In this light, mentorship is not just a beneficial activity but a necessary endeavor for national and continental development. By prioritizing the support of mentorship initiatives, governments and the AU can ensure that Africa's youth are equipped, empowered, and inspired to contribute to their societies in meaningful ways, driving sustainable development and fostering a brighter future for the continent.

As we wrap up the discussion on the pivotal role of governments and the African Union in supporting mentorship, it's clear that their involvement is crucial, far beyond just being beneficial. Their ability to establish supportive policies, allocate necessary resources, and provide visionary leadership uniquely positions them to significantly enhance the scope and effectiveness of mentorship programs across Africa.

This analysis has highlighted the transformative potential of such support, turning mentorship from a series of localized efforts into major catalysts for social development and stability. By nurturing Africa's human capital and fostering an environment conducive to innovation and entrepreneurship, and by ensuring these efforts are in line with Sustainable Development Goals, these governmental bodies can make mentorship a key element of positive change.

The benefits of this support extend well beyond the immediate impacts on mentees. They contribute to broader societal advantages, helping to steer Africa towards sustainable development and enhancing its competitiveness on the global stage. As Africa continues to progress, the argument for not just continuing but also significantly increasing support for mentorship initiatives becomes compelling.

Incorporating mentorship as a core element of development strategies offers a forward-thinking approach to empowering the continent's future leaders, innovators, and change-makers. Thus, the ongoing and expanded commitment to mentorship should be seen as both a strategic necessity and a moral imperative, essential for securing a thriving, prosperous future for Africa and its people. This approach ensures that mentorship remains a cornerstone for building a resilient, dynamic Africa capable of meeting the challenges and seizing the opportunities of the future.

PARTNERSHIPS AND COLLABORATION

The concept of partnerships and collaboration within African mentorship programs is integral to magnifying their reach and efficacy. Strategic alliances among diverse stakeholders —governments, NGOs, the private sector, and local communities— significantly enhance the sustainability and impact of mentorship initiatives across the continent.

In Africa, where diverse challenges can impede the progress of mentorship programs, the synergy from collaborations proves invaluable. By uniting the unique resources and strengths of various sectors, these partnerships can address logistical hurdles, bridge resource gaps, and navigate cultural complexities more effectively than any single organization could alone. This cooperative approach not only broadens the scope of mentorship programs but also enriches them, providing a robust support network for the youth.

For instance, government agencies can offer policy support and funding, NGOs can bring on-ground insights and innovative methodologies, the private sector can contribute expertise and additional resources, and local communities can ensure that programs are culturally aligned and widely accepted. Together, these entities create a comprehensive ecosystem that supports the holistic development of young individuals.

This collaboration also cultivates a shared commitment to youth empowerment, which is crucial for fostering long-term societal benefits. When diverse groups unite with a common purpose, it reinforces the mentorship programs' roles in promoting education, professional development, and entrepreneurial endeavors among Africa's youth. This unity not only accelerates the personal growth of individuals but also propels societal advancement.

Successful examples of such collaborations showcase how joint efforts have led to scalable and impactful mentorship models. These models illustrate how strategic partnerships can overcome substantial challenges, making mentorship accessible to a larger number of young Africans. Additionally, these collaborations offer insights into best practices for initiating and sustaining partnerships, ensuring they remain effective and mutually beneficial over time.

One case in point is a collaboration where a government agency provided policy support and funding, an NGO offered innovative training methods, a private company shared industry-specific expertise, and local community leaders ensured cultural relevance and community buy-in. This joint effort resulted in a mentorship program that not only thrived but also became a model for others to follow.

Ultimately, the integration of partnerships and collaboration in mentorship programs represents a powerful strategy for enhancing the developmental trajectory of Africa's youth and, by extension, advancing the continent's broader goals of growth and stability. Through detailed exploration and real-world case studies, the importance of collective action in the realm of mentorship becomes clear, highlighting how it is not just beneficial but essential for fostering a prosperous and stable African society. By working together, these diverse groups can create mentorship initiatives that have a lasting, transformative impact on the lives of young Africans and their communities.

Collaborating With Governments, Ngos, And The Private Sector

Mentorship programs in Africa, when synergized through collaborations between governments, non-governmental organizations (NGOs), and the private sector, can profoundly enhance the capabilities and opportunities available to the continent's youth. These partnerships are essential, leveraging distinct strengths and resources across the public, non-profit, and private sectors to build comprehensive, sustainable mentorship ecosystems that contribute significantly to both individual and societal development.

Governments provide a structural backbone for mentorship initiatives through policy, funding, and infrastructural support. By integrating mentorship into national youth policies and educational frameworks, governments can ensure these programs align with broader development goals, such as reducing unemployment or enhancing technical skills among the youth. For instance, governmental support can facilitate the scale and reach of mentorship programs by providing access to schools, community centers, and public institutions, where these programs can be administered.

NGOs play a crucial role in tailoring mentorship programs to meet specific local needs, offering flexibility and specialized knowledge that governmental bodies might not possess. Their close ties to communities allow them to implement mentorship initiatives that are culturally sensitive and locally relevant. NGOs like SAYes Youth Mentoring in South Africa exemplify this by providing targeted mentorship to youths transitioning out of childcare systems, effectively preparing them for independent adult life by focusing on practical life skills and employment readiness.

The involvement of the private sector introduces a practical, hands-on perspective to mentorship, especially valuable in areas like entrepreneurship and industry-specific skills training. Companies can provide mentors from within their ranks, who bring industry insights, career development advice, and potential professional networking opportunities that are invaluable for young mentees. Moreover, through Corporate Social Responsibility (CSR) initiatives, businesses can invest in the community by supporting mentorship programs, which in turn helps develop a future workforce better prepared for the challenges of the modern economic landscape.

The combined efforts of these sectors not only enhance the reach and quality of mentorship programs but also ensure they are sustainable and impactful. Collaborative efforts can overcome significant challenges such as funding shortages, lack of mentor availability, and program reach, making mentorship accessible to a broader audience. Moreover, these partnerships can foster innovation in mentorship practices by integrating various perspectives and resources, from digital tools provided by tech companies to research and monitoring frameworks that can be supported by academic institutions.

The strategic collaboration among governments, NGOs, and the private sector is vital for the success of mentorship programs in Africa. Each partner brings unique strengths that, when combined, provide a robust support system for the continent's youth, equipping them with the necessary tools to succeed personally and professionally. Such partnerships not only prepare individuals for immediate challenges but also foster long-term societal benefits by cultivating a well-rounded, skilled, and resilient youth population poised to lead Africa toward a prosperous future.

Through these collaborative efforts, mentorship becomes a powerful catalyst for widespread societal change and development, underscoring the importance of continued and enhanced support from all sectors of society. This multifaceted approach ensures that mentorship programs can adapt and thrive, addressing the diverse and evolving needs of African youth while contributing to the broader goals of economic growth, social cohesion, and sustainable development. By working together, these sectors can create a lasting impact that resonates across generations, helping to build a brighter and more equitable future for all.

Building Effective Networks For Sustainable Mentorship

Building effective networks for sustainable mentorship is a multifaceted endeavor that requires deliberate strategy, commitment, and collaboration among various stakeholders. The essence of creating a thriving mentorship ecosystem lies in the ability to forge partnerships that are not only strategic but also synergistic, ensuring that the collective effort is greater than the sum of its parts. This exploration delves into creating collaborative frameworks, highlights successful case studies of partnerships, and addresses common challenges faced in collaboration, providing a comprehensive guide to building networks that can sustain and enhance mentorship programs across Africa.

The foundation of any successful mentorship network is a collaborative framework that aligns the goals, resources, and strengths of all involved parties. This framework should facilitate open communication, shared objectives, and mutual benefits, ensuring that each stakeholder is invested in the success of the mentorship initiative. Strategies for creating such a framework include identifying and engaging key stakeholders early to garner support and identify mutual interests. Establishing clear goals and expectations collaboratively defines the objectives of the mentorship program and the role each partner will play. This clarity prevents misunderstandings and ensures all efforts are aligned towards a common goal. Facilitating resource sharing through mechanisms like pooled funds or co-hosted training sessions can make resources go further and benefit a broader audience. Regular communication and structured feedback among partners are essential for keeping the network active and responsive to any issues or opportunities that arise.

Successful partnerships serve as blueprints for what is possible when different entities come together in support of mentorship. For instance, in Kenya, a collaboration between the government's youth development agency and a major telecommunications company leveraged corporate resources for a digital mentorship platform that significantly broadened youth access to mentorship programs. In Ghana, a partnership between an international NGO and local universities has developed programs supporting female students in STEM fields, showing how targeted collaborations can address specific community needs and promote inclusion.

While the benefits of collaboration are significant, partnerships can face challenges that hinder their effectiveness. Diverging objectives among stakeholders, difficulties in resource allocation, and challenges in maintaining sustained engagement are common.

Strategies to overcome these challenges include aligning visions and objectives through workshops and strategy sessions to ensure mutual understanding and purpose. Establishing transparent resource management practices builds trust and accountability, crucial for sustaining long-term partnerships. Fostering a culture of commitment and adapting to evolving needs as the program develops are also vital for keeping collaborations effective and responsive to the changing landscape of mentorship needs.

Building effective networks for sustainable mentorship involves more than just connecting individuals and organizations; it requires a strategic vision that embraces flexibility, commitment, and a deep understanding of the varied needs across different regions and communities in Africa. Through thoughtful planning and robust collaboration, these networks can support impactful mentorship initiatives that contribute significantly to the development of the continent's youth and the broader societal goals of African nations. This comprehensive approach ensures that mentorship programs are not only effective in meeting immediate needs but are also sustainable over the long term, adapting to new challenges and opportunities as they arise.

The significance of partnerships and collaborations in the realm of mentorship programs across Africa cannot be overstated. The success of these programs, designed to foster the growth and development of the continent's youth, depends critically on robust, multi-faceted partnerships that span governmental bodies, non-governmental organizations (NGOs), private sector entities, and community organizations. Such collaborations are fundamental, not only for broadening the reach of mentorship initiatives but also for deepening their impact, ensuring they deliver tangible benefits to their participants.

These partnerships facilitate a pooling of resources, expertise, and networks, each bringing unique strengths to the table, thus enabling mentorship programs to overcome challenges that might otherwise be insurmountable. For instance, government involvement can provide mentorship programs with essential policy support and access to public resources, while the private sector can contribute innovation and practical career opportunities for mentees. NGOs play a critical role in bridging the gap between these large entities and the communities they serve, ensuring that programs are tailored to meet the specific needs of different demographic groups.

Successful case studies from across Africa show that when these entities work together under a shared vision for youth empowerment and development, the results can be transformative. These collaborations not only amplify individual efforts but create synergies that can significantly enhance the quality and sustainability of mentorship initiatives. By integrating efforts, sharing expertise, and aligning goals, stakeholders can create a mentorship ecosystem that is more resilient and effective.

However, building these networks is not without its challenges. Differences in objectives, bureaucratic red tape, and resource allocation issues can impede effective collaboration. Overcoming these challenges requires clear communication, mutual respect for each partner's contributions, and a commitment to shared outcomes. Regular interaction and feedback mechanisms are essential in ensuring that all parties remain aligned and responsive to the evolving needs of the mentorship programs.

Creating and maintaining effective networks for sustainable mentorship programs in Africa demands a concerted effort from a diverse array of stakeholders. Governments, NGOs, the private sector, and community organizations must come together, each contributing their unique strengths and resources. By doing so, they can build robust, adaptable, and impactful mentorship networks that not only meet the immediate needs of young people but also foster long-term societal benefits. Through strategic partnerships, clear communication, and a shared commitment to youth development, these networks can become powerful engines of positive change, driving Africa towards a more prosperous and stable future.

The path forward must focus on strengthening these partnerships, encouraging even greater collaboration and resource sharing to support Africa's youth effectively. By doing so, stakeholders can ensure that mentorship remains a dynamic force for good, capable of empowering young individuals and, consequently, fostering broader societal development and stability. This collective approach will not only support the current generation but will also set a precedent for how collaborative efforts can tackle complex challenges across the continent.

When diverse entities—governments, NGOs, the private sector, and community organizations—unite under a common goal, the impact of mentorship programs can be exponentially greater. Such partnerships create a rich tapestry of support, weaving together varied resources and expertise to build mentorship initiatives that are both resilient and far-reaching. By pooling their strengths, these collaborators can overcome logistical hurdles, bridge resource gaps, and navigate cultural complexities with greater efficacy than any single entity could achieve alone.

Furthermore, the integration of different perspectives and experiences within these partnerships fosters innovation and adaptability. As mentorship programs evolve to meet the changing needs of Africa's youth, the ability to draw on a diverse pool of knowledge and resources becomes invaluable. This adaptability ensures that mentorship initiatives remain relevant, impactful, and capable of addressing emerging challenges head-on.

Stakeholders must remain committed to open communication, shared objectives, and continuous improvement to maintain the vitality of these partnerships. Regular interaction and feedback loops will help to align efforts, foster trust, and adapt strategies as needed. Through sustained collaboration, mentorship programs can continue to grow and thrive, making a lasting difference in the lives of young Africans and the communities they belong to.

The future of Africa's youth depends on these collaborative efforts. By championing partnership and cooperation, stakeholders can create a robust support system that empowers young individuals to achieve their full potential. This, in turn, will drive economic growth, social cohesion, and sustainable development across the continent. The power of mentorship, amplified through strategic alliances, holds the key to unlocking a brighter, more equitable future for Africa and its next generation of leaders.

THE ROLE OF AFRICAN DIASPORA IN MENTORSHIP

The influence of the African diaspora on mentorship within Africa offers a potent mix of local relevance and global perspective that is pivotal for the continent's socio-economic development. The diaspora, with its diverse experiences and broadened horizons, brings valuable cross-cultural insights and a wealth of global knowledge that are integral to nurturing the continent's next generation of leaders.

Members of the African diaspora, spread across the globe, maintain strong ties to their roots, with many seeking to contribute meaningfully back to their home countries. Their unique position allows them to bridge the gap between the international scene and local realities, providing mentorship that is culturally attuned yet expansive in scope. This dual perspective enables diaspora mentors to guide African youth not only within local contexts but also in understanding and navigating global arenas. For instance, diaspora professionals can offer African mentees insights into industries and career paths that are well-established abroad but nascent in Africa, such as certain technology sectors.

Moreover, these mentors often bring extensive international networks that can open significant doors for young Africans. These networks facilitate exchanges that can lead to internships, study opportunities, and collaborations with both educational and corporate institutions abroad. Such connections are invaluable, providing young people with access to new ideas, cutting-edge technologies, and alternative business models, all of which can be adapted and applied within their home countries.

The role of technology in diaspora-led mentorship cannot be understated. Through digital platforms, mentors and mentees can connect across continents in real time, making geographical distance irrelevant. Initiatives like virtual workshops, webinars, and online coaching sessions are becoming increasingly common, allowing for consistent interaction and engagement without the need for physical presence.

By participating in mentorship, the diaspora not only enriches the lives of individual mentees but also contributes to the broader development goals of African nations. These efforts align with broader social aims such as enhancing education, reducing unemployment, and fostering economic growth.

The role of the African diaspora in mentorship highlights not just the personal benefits for the mentees but also the transformative potential for societal advancement. It reflects a powerful trend toward leveraging global African networks to foster development and empowerment across the continent, underscoring the profound impact of nurturing such connections for the future of Africa. By embracing this dynamic, the diaspora helps to create a robust pipeline of skilled, knowledgeable, and globally aware leaders ready to drive Africa's progress in the 21st century.

Defining The African Diaspora: Scope, Identity, And Connection

The African diaspora represents a global community of people of African descent living outside the African continent, whether by choice, coercion, or necessity. This expansive network spans across continents, encompassing individuals and communities in the Americas, Europe, Asia, and beyond. The diaspora's scope is vast, including descendants of the transatlantic slave trade, recent migrants, and those who have settled in other regions for educational or professional reasons. Despite the geographical separation, a shared heritage and a sense of connection to Africa unite the diaspora.

The African diaspora's roots are deeply intertwined with the history of human civilization. From ancient migrations to the forced exodus during the transatlantic slave trade, and more recent waves of migration for economic, educational, or political reasons, the movements of African peoples have shaped cultures and societies around the world. Each wave of migration has added layers to the diaspora's identity, blending African traditions with local cultures and creating rich, multifaceted communities that reflect the diversity of the African experience.

The identity of the African diaspora is a rich tapestry woven from a myriad of historical, cultural, and social threads. This complex and dynamic identity transcends simple definitions, embodying a broad spectrum of experiences, languages, and traditions that contribute to a vibrant mosaic of global African culture. It's important to clarify that when we discuss the African diaspora in the context of mentorship and social change, we are not defining African identity by color or race. Rather, we recognize the multifaceted nature of this identity, shaped by diverse experiences and contributions across the globe.

Members of the African diaspora navigate multiple layers of identity, balancing their intrinsic African heritage with the cultural norms and societal expectations of their host countries. This balancing act grants them a unique perspective, allowing them to foster a deep understanding of cross-cultural dynamics. Such insights are invaluable in mentorship, where understanding and empathy are crucial to forming meaningful connections and providing relevant guidance.

This nuanced understanding of identity enriches the diaspora's contributions to mentorship and development initiatives. Their global perspective, coupled with an inherent connection to African heritage, positions members of the diaspora as bridge-builders. They are uniquely equipped to facilitate cross-cultural exchanges, share diverse insights, and apply global knowledge to local contexts. In mentorship programs, this enables the design and implementation of culturally sensitive approaches that resonate with mentees' experiences and aspirations.

Moreover, the African diaspora's engagement in mentorship extends the reach and impact of these programs, connecting continents and communities in a shared effort to foster growth, leadership, and innovation. Their contributions underscore the importance of embracing a broad, inclusive view of African identity, recognizing the rich diversity and potential within the global African community. Through mentorship, members of the diaspora play a pivotal role in nurturing the next generation of leaders and innovators, contributing significantly to the tapestry of social change across Africa and beyond.

Despite physical distance, the African diaspora maintains strong ties to the continent. These connections are manifested in various forms, including remittances, which play a significant role in the economies of many African countries, cultural exchanges that promote African arts and traditions globally, and advocacy efforts that highlight issues affecting Africa on the world stage. Furthermore, the diaspora's engagement in mentorship and development initiatives underscores a commitment to Africa's growth, leveraging global experiences and networks to support education, entrepreneurship, and social innovation on the continent.

Today, the African diaspora is recognized as a key stakeholder in Africa's development. The diaspora's potential to influence economic growth, political reform, and social change is increasingly acknowledged by policymakers and development practitioners. Through mentorship, the diaspora imparts valuable skills and knowledge, nurtures innovation, and fosters a generation of leaders equipped to address the challenges and seize the opportunities of the 21st century. The diaspora's involvement in mentorship initiatives exemplifies a broader trend of leveraging global networks for local impact, contributing to a vision of a prosperous, interconnected Africa.

The African diaspora's scope, identity, and enduring connection to the African continent are central to understanding its role in mentorship and development. By bridging cultures, sharing global experiences, and maintaining strong ties to Africa, the diaspora enriches the mentorship landscape and contributes significantly to the continent's development. As we explore the contributions of the African diaspora, it becomes clear that their global perspective, combined with a deep-rooted connection to Africa, is a powerful force for positive change, driving forward mentorship initiatives that are vital for Africa's future.

Bridging Global Opportunities And Local Needs

The African diaspora, a vast network of people of African descent living outside the continent, plays a pivotal role in bridging global opportunities with local needs in Africa. This community, leveraging its broad international presence and expertise, uniquely tailors mentorship programs to meet the localized challenges of the continent while introducing global standards and opportunities, particularly in education, entrepreneurship, and technology.

Diaspora-led mentorship programs significantly enhance the educational landscape in Africa by connecting local students and professionals with global educational resources. These programs often facilitate access to scholarships, advanced online courses, and international academic networks, enriching the local educational offerings. For example, through these mentorships, students in Africa can receive guidance on applying to foreign universities, gaining access to cutting-edge research opportunities, or engaging in exchange programs that broaden their academic and cultural horizons. This not only helps to elevate the educational standards by filling in gaps in local systems but also prepares students for competitive roles globally.

In the economic sector, diaspora mentors are instrumental in nurturing entrepreneurial spirit by linking African entrepreneurs with international markets, investment opportunities, and business strategies crucial for scaling operations globally. They provide insights into market dynamics, help navigate regulatory environments, and connect young businesses with potential international investors. This mentorship drives innovation and job creation, essential for the continent's economic growth and stability.

The technology sector, perhaps more than any other, benefits immensely from the diaspora's mentorship. Members of the diaspora use their positions within global tech industries to facilitate knowledge and technology transfer to the African continent. They mentor young professionals in skills related to emerging technologies such as artificial intelligence, cybersecurity, and renewable energy, helping integrate these into local markets and operations. Additionally, they connect mentees with global tech networks, fostering collaborations that can lead to innovative projects and startups in Africa.

The engagement of the African diaspora in mentorship is transformative, creating a valuable link between African youths and the global stage. This connection is crucial for bringing contemporary skills and new perspectives to the continent, while also ensuring that the youth can compete on an international level. Through such mentorship, the diaspora not only fosters local talent but also contributes to the socio-economic development of the continent, helping to realize a vision of an empowered, progressive, and self-sustaining Africa.

Ultimately, the success of these diaspora-led initiatives showcases the significant impact of leveraging global networks for local development. It highlights the critical role of cultural and professional exchanges in driving economic growth, technological advancement, and educational excellence in Africa. This approach not only prepares the continent's youth for future challenges but also ensures that Africa can harness its full potential in the increasingly interconnected global landscape.

Cross-Cultural Exchange And Understanding

Cross-cultural exchange and understanding lie at the heart of mentorship initiatives led by the African diaspora, serving as a bridge that connects the rich cultural heritage of Africa with the diverse tapestry of global cultures. This exchange is more than just a transfer of knowledge or skills; it's a dialogue that fosters mutual respect, broadens perspectives, and enriches both mentors and mentees with a deeper appreciation of the world's cultural diversity. Such mentorship programs are instrumental in preparing African mentees for the global stage, equipping them with the competencies needed to navigate, contribute to, and excel in a connected world.

The diaspora's unique position, straddling their African heritage and their experiences in other cultural contexts, enables them to impart crucial global competencies to their mentees. This includes intercultural communication skills, adaptability, and an understanding of global professional standards and practices. Through mentorship, mentees can learn not only to appreciate and navigate cultural differences but also to leverage these differences as strengths in their professional and personal lives.

Mentorship programs facilitate a two-way exchange of cultural values and perspectives that enriches the mentorship experience. Mentees gain insights into the cultural nuances of their mentors' adopted countries, including workplace norms, societal values, and professional etiquettes that are critical for success in international environments. Conversely, mentors learn from the local knowledge, traditions, and perspectives of their mentees, fostering a deeper connection to their roots and an appreciation of Africa's contribution to global diversity. This exchange often leads to a profound transformation in how mentees perceive their place in the world. By understanding the interconnectedness of cultures and the value of diverse perspectives, they are better prepared to engage in global dialogues, collaborations, and initiatives.

The mentorship also extends to the sharing of global professional practices, preparing mentees for careers that may span international borders. Mentors provide guidance on navigating the global job market, including resume preparation for international roles, interview techniques that resonate across cultures, and strategies for building a global professional network. This preparation is invaluable for mentees looking to pursue opportunities abroad or within multinational companies operating in Africa. Moreover, the mentorship experience often inspires mentees to seek out global experiences of their own, whether through study, work, or travel, further enriching their understanding and appreciation of cross-cultural dynamics.

The cross-cultural exchange and understanding facilitated by mentorship programs led by the African diaspora are invaluable components of preparing Africa's youth for the global stage. By bridging cultural divides and fostering a mutual exchange of values, perspectives, and professional practices, these programs enhance the global competency of African mentees. This not only prepares them for success in a multicultural world but also contributes to a richer, more inclusive global community. The diaspora's role in this process underscores the importance of leveraging global networks and experiences for the benefit of the continent, showcasing the power of mentorship as a tool for cross-cultural understanding and global engagement.

These mentorship programs foster a unique synergy, merging the richness of African culture with the dynamism of global experiences, ultimately preparing young Africans to thrive in an interconnected world. The impact of such cross-cultural mentorship is profound, cultivating a generation of leaders who are not only rooted in their heritage but also equipped to navigate and influence the global landscape. This blend of local and global perspectives ensures that Africa's youth are well-prepared to contribute meaningfully to both their communities and the world at large.

Leveraging International Networks For Development

The African diaspora's mentorship initiatives can serve as a critical conduit, connecting African mentees to a broader world of opportunities, insights, and collaborations. By leveraging their international networks, diaspora mentors provide African mentees with unparalleled access to global markets, strategic partnerships, and educational opportunities that can dramatically reshape their career paths and entrepreneurial ventures. This leveraging of international networks underscores the potential of mentorship to transcend local boundaries, fostering development that is both locally grounded and globally informed.

For many African entrepreneurs and professionals, the global market represents a vast landscape of opportunities yet to be explored. Diaspora mentors, with their understanding of both local African contexts and international market dynamics, are uniquely positioned to guide mentees in navigating this complex terrain. They can offer insights into consumer behavior, market trends, and regulatory environments across different regions, enabling mentees to tailor their products and services to meet global standards and demands. This mentorship can transform local ventures into competitive players on the international stage, opening new avenues for growth and revenue.

One of the most valuable assets that diaspora mentors can bring to their mentees is access to international networks of professionals, investors, and collaborators. These connections can lead to strategic partnerships that enhance the mentees' ventures in terms of technology transfer, funding, and market access. For instance, a mentor with connections in the tech industry can introduce a mentee developing an innovative app to potential investors or partners abroad, significantly accelerating the project's development and launch. Similarly, mentors can connect mentees with academic and research institutions, paving the way for collaborative projects that bolster innovation and development.

Beyond professional and entrepreneurial development, diaspora mentors can play a pivotal role in connecting African mentees to educational opportunities abroad. This includes scholarships, internships, and exchange programs that provide mentees with exposure to international best practices, advanced technologies, and new cultural perspectives. Such experiences are invaluable, equipping mentees with the skills, knowledge, and global outlook necessary for success in an interconnected world. Furthermore, these educational opportunities often come with professional networks that mentees can leverage long after their programs have concluded, offering ongoing support and guidance throughout their careers.

The power of international networks in driving development cannot be overstated. Through mentorship, the diaspora not only shares its knowledge and experience but also opens doors that many African mentees might not have access to otherwise. These networks act as bridges, connecting African talent with global opportunities, fostering an environment where innovation, collaboration, and growth can flourish. Moreover, as mentees progress in their careers and ventures, they too become part of these international networks, further expanding the reach and impact of the diaspora's mentorship efforts. This cyclical growth enhances the mentorship ecosystem, ensuring its sustainability and continued relevance.

Leveraging international networks through diaspora-led mentorship represents a powerful mechanism for catalyzing development in Africa. By providing African mentees with access to global markets, strategic partnerships, and educational opportunities, mentorship initiatives are not just guiding individual careers but are shaping the continent's future. These networks are invaluable resources, opening doors to experiences, collaborations, and insights that enrich the mentees' professional and personal development. Through this global engagement, mentorship emerges as a key driver of not just individual success but broader socio-economic progress, showcasing the transformative power of connectedness in the modern world.

Remittances As Investment In Mentorship

The role of the African diaspora in the continent's development has traditionally been linked to remittances, with billions of dollars sent home annually to support families and communities. However, a transformative shift is occurring in how these remittances are viewed and utilized. Increasingly, members of the diaspora are channeling their remittances into strategic investments that foster long-term development and empowerment. This innovative approach sees remittances not just as financial aid but as capital for mentorship programs, educational initiatives, and social enterprises. This shift towards investing remittances in mentorship is catalyzing sustainable development and creating a broader societal impact.

One of the most impactful ways the diaspora utilizes remittances is by funding educational initiatives. These investments often support scholarships, school infrastructure projects, and technology access programs, directly contributing to the enhancement of educational quality and accessibility. By targeting education, these remittances help cultivate a fertile ground for mentorship, where young Africans are better prepared and more accessible for guidance and growth opportunities. Such investments ensure that the benefits of mentorship can reach a wider audience, laying the foundation for a more educated, empowered generation.

Another significant avenue for the investment of remittances is in start-ups and social enterprises led by young African entrepreneurs. Diaspora members, leveraging their global insights and networks, provide not only the capital but also mentorship to these ventures. This dual support accelerates the growth of start-ups, driving innovation and job creation within local economies. Moreover, social enterprises that address community challenges—such as access to clean water, healthcare, and sustainable agriculture—receive a much-needed boost from these investments. Through this approach, remittances serve as seed money for projects with the potential for wide-reaching social impact, embodying the spirit of mentorship by fostering environments where community-driven solutions can thrive.

Direct investment in mentorship programs is perhaps the most direct manifestation of remittances as a tool for empowerment. These funds support the creation and expansion of mentorship initiatives that connect experienced diaspora members with mentees back home. Investments might cover operational costs, training materials, and technology platforms that facilitate cross-border mentorship relationships. By financially backing these programs, the diaspora ensures that mentorship is accessible to a broader segment of the population, including those in underserved or remote areas. This strategic use of remittances amplifies the impact of mentorship, turning it into a scalable tool for personal and professional development across the continent.

This shift towards viewing remittances as investments in mentorship and development reflects a deeper understanding of the role the diaspora can play in Africa's future. It signifies a move from short-term financial support to long-term development strategies that leverage education, entrepreneurship, and mentorship for societal impact. This approach not only maximizes the utility of remittances but also aligns with a broader vision of empowerment and sustainable growth. It embodies a commitment to nurturing the potential of African youth, ensuring that the benefits of these investments ripple through communities and generations.

The strategic investment of remittances in mentorship, educational initiatives, and social enterprises represents a paradigm shift in the diaspora's contribution to Africa's development. By channeling financial resources into programs that build capacity, foster innovation, and empower young leaders, the diaspora is leveraging its unique position to effect meaningful change. This innovative approach to remittances underscores the importance of mentorship as a tool for development, highlighting the transformative potential of these investments to shape a brighter future for the continent. Through such strategic contributions, the diaspora plays a pivotal role in driving sustainable development and nurturing the next generation of African leaders and innovators.

As we continue to harness the power of remittances for broader developmental goals, it's evident that these financial contributions, when strategically invested, can create a ripple effect of positive change. The diaspora's involvement in mentorship and other developmental initiatives is not just beneficial; it's essential for the sustainable growth and empowerment of Africa. This evolving perspective on remittances heralds a new era of development, where financial support is seamlessly integrated with capacity building and long-term growth strategies.

Technology-Enabled Mentorship Platforms

The advent of technology-enabled mentorship platforms has revolutionized the way mentorship is conducted, particularly in bridging the gap between the African diaspora and mentees on the continent. These digital platforms leverage the power of the internet and mobile technology to overcome geographical barriers, making it possible for mentors and mentees to connect, communicate, and collaborate across vast distances. This exploration delves into the innovative ways through which the diaspora utilizes technology to foster mentorship relationships, highlighting the features, benefits, and impacts of these platforms.

One of the key innovations in technology-enabled mentorship is the development of platforms that specifically cater to the needs of the African context. These platforms are designed to be accessible, user-friendly, and relevant to the challenges and opportunities present within the continent. They offer various tools and resources, including video conferencing, messaging, project collaboration spaces, and resource libraries, ensuring that mentors and mentees can engage in meaningful mentorship activities despite being miles apart.

Technology-enabled mentorship platforms are revolutionizing how mentorship is delivered, particularly in connecting the African diaspora with mentees across the continent. These platforms leverage digital tools to facilitate mentorship that is not only effective but also expansive, reaching across geographical and cultural barriers.

Video conferencing is crucial for making mentorship sessions more personal and engaging. It allows for face-to-face interaction, which enhances the quality of communication and builds stronger relationships between mentors and mentees. This real-time connection can simulate a classroom or office meeting environment, providing a space for lively discussions, immediate feedback, and more nuanced understanding.

Messaging and communication tools are essential in any mentorship relationship. Modern platforms incorporate messaging features that allow mentors and mentees to maintain constant contact. This facilitates the flow of information, allows for quick feedback, and supports the building of rapport. Mentees can ask questions as they arise and receive timely advice, making the mentorship process more fluid and responsive to their needs.

Collaborative workspaces are digital environments where documents can be shared, edited, and discussed. This feature supports a hands-on learning experience, which is vital for projects that require collaboration, such as business planning or academic research. Collaborative workspaces help track progress and ensure that both mentors and mentees are on the same page, literally and metaphorically.

Access to comprehensive resource libraries is another significant advantage of technology-enabled mentorship platforms. These libraries often contain educational materials, recorded webinars, and workshops, which can significantly enrich the mentorship experience. They provide mentees with additional learning opportunities that can complement the guidance provided by their mentors.

Diaspora Connect is an example of a successful platform that specializes in connecting African entrepreneurs with mentors from the diaspora in the business and technology sectors. It facilitates mentorship in critical areas such as business strategy and technological innovation and includes success stories that serve as motivation and learning tools for new entrepreneurs. EduBridge focuses on academic mentorship, linking African students with academic professionals worldwide. EduBridge offers support for academic projects, career counseling, and information about scholarship opportunities, enhancing students' educational experiences and career prospects.

The impact of these technology-enabled platforms extends beyond individual mentorship relationships. They provide mentees with unprecedented access to global networks of knowledge and professional opportunities. For mentors, these platforms offer a flexible and impactful way to engage with and contribute to the development of their home countries.

Moreover, these platforms help foster a community among users, which is crucial for creating a supportive network committed to mutual growth and development. They also underscore the significant role of the African diaspora in the continent's developmental narrative, showcasing how technological advancements can facilitate impactful cross-border engagement and support.

As technology continues to advance, the potential for these platforms to expand and deepen their impact grows. They are proving to be not only tools for individual development but also catalysts for broader social and economic progress across Africa. This new era of digital mentorship is transforming the landscape of mentorship, making it more inclusive, accessible, and effective in nurturing the next generation of African leaders and innovators.

Capacity Building And Skills Transfer

The diaspora's role in fostering development within Africa extends significantly through efforts in capacity building and skills transfer.

Armed with global experiences, advanced skills, and a wealth of professional knowledge, members of the African diaspora are uniquely positioned to catalyze change and drive progress within their home countries. By engaging in mentorship, they impart critical competencies and professional insights that are instrumental in shaping the continent's burgeoning talent pool. This exploration illuminates the profound impact of such diaspora-led initiatives, showcasing successful instances where capacity building and skills transfer have transformed local communities and empowered African mentees.

One of the most impactful areas of diaspora engagement is in entrepreneurship training and business development. Through mentorship programs, diaspora members transfer essential business skills, including financial literacy, marketing strategies, and operational management, to budding entrepreneurs in Africa. An exemplary initiative in this realm is the "African Business Mentorship Program" (ABMP), which pairs diaspora professionals with SME owners and startup founders. The ABMP has been instrumental in scaling small businesses, improving their market competitiveness, and increasing their sustainability. Mentees under the program have reported significant growth in revenue, expansion into new markets, and increased employment opportunities within their businesses.

The diaspora also plays a pivotal role in transferring technical skills and fostering innovation, particularly in fields like technology, engineering, and healthcare. "TechBridge Africa," for instance, connects African tech enthusiasts with diaspora mentors in Silicon Valley and other global tech hubs. Through this platform, mentees gain insights into the latest technological advancements, coding skills, and project management techniques. Success stories from TechBridge Africa include mentees launching successful tech startups, developing community-based tech solutions, and securing positions with leading technology firms.

Beyond entrepreneurship and technical skills, the diaspora contributes significantly to educational capacity building. Initiatives such as "Diaspora Educators Network" (DEN) see African academics and professionals abroad volunteering their time to teach courses, conduct workshops, and provide academic mentorship via virtual platforms. This engagement has enriched educational experiences for students in Africa, offering them exposure to global perspectives, advanced curricula, and research opportunities that are otherwise scarce. The DEN has facilitated partnerships between African universities and institutions abroad, enhancing academic standards and broadening the scope of educational offerings on the continent.

In the healthcare sector, diaspora professionals have initiated mentorship programs aimed at transferring critical medical knowledge and skills. Programs like "Health for Africa" leverage the expertise of African doctors and healthcare professionals living abroad to mentor medical students and healthcare workers in rural communities. These mentorship engagements cover a wide range of topics, from clinical skills and patient care to healthcare management and public health strategies. The impact of these programs is profound, contributing to improved healthcare delivery, enhanced patient outcomes, and the overall strengthening of local healthcare systems.

The capacity building and skills transfer facilitated by the African diaspora represent a powerful tool for development, directly impacting professional growth, entrepreneurship, innovation, and education within the continent. By sharing their acquired skills and professional experiences, diaspora mentors not only enhance the competencies of individual mentees but also contribute to the broader goal of sustainable development in Africa. These successful instances of diaspora engagement underscore the potential of mentorship and collaboration to transform local communities, empower the next generation, and shape a prosperous future for Africa.

Through these initiatives, the diaspora demonstrates its unwavering commitment to Africa's development. The ripple effect of their efforts is felt across various sectors, driving progress and fostering a culture of continuous learning and innovation. This dynamic exchange of knowledge and skills is pivotal in creating a resilient, self-sustaining Africa where the youth are equipped to lead and innovate. The stories of success from these mentorship programs illustrate the transformative power of the diaspora's involvement, highlighting the significant impact that can be achieved through dedicated and strategic capacity building.

Challenges And Opportunities

The diaspora's engagement in mentorship within Africa, though rich with potential for transformative impact, is not without its challenges. Logistical complexities, cultural nuances, and the quest for reliable local partnerships present hurdles that can complicate mentorship efforts. However, within these challenges lie significant opportunities for innovation, deeper engagement, and the strengthening of mentorship initiatives. This exploration delves into the multifaceted nature of these challenges and outlines strategies for leveraging them as opportunities to cultivate more meaningful and sustainable mentorship relationships.

Navigating logistical challenges of coordinating mentorship activities across different time zones, geographical distances, and technological barriers are significant. However, these challenges prompt the adoption of innovative solutions such as flexible scheduling, the use of versatile digital platforms, and the development of mobile applications tailored to mentorship needs. These adaptations not only overcome logistical hurdles but also enhance the accessibility and inclusivity of mentorship programs, ensuring that more individuals can benefit from diaspora expertise regardless of their location.

Potential cultural disconnects between diaspora mentors and African mentees can affect the depth and effectiveness of mentorship relationships. Yet, this challenge offers an opportunity to foster cross-cultural exchange and understanding. By incorporating cultural competency training into mentorship programs, both mentors and mentees can gain insights into each other's cultural contexts, enhancing mutual respect and communication. This approach enriches the mentorship experience, turning cultural diversity into a strength that broadens perspectives and fosters global awareness among participants.

The search for reliable local partners to facilitate mentorship initiatives on the ground can be daunting. However, this challenge presents an opportunity to build strong networks and collaborations with local educational institutions, businesses, and community organizations. Establishing these partnerships not only aids in the effective implementation of mentorship programs but also ensures that these initiatives are grounded in local needs and realities. Furthermore, working closely with local partners enhances the sustainability of mentorship efforts, creating a robust foundation for long-term impact.

The diversity within the African diaspora itself—spanning various professions, industries, and experiences—while challenging in terms of program coordination, offers a rich reservoir of knowledge and perspectives. By effectively harnessing this diversity, mentorship programs can offer a wide range of expertise and mentorship opportunities, tailored to the varied interests and needs of African mentees. This approach maximizes the impact of diaspora involvement, providing mentees with access to a broad spectrum of mentors who can guide them in multiple areas of personal and professional development.

The challenges associated with diaspora-led mentorship in Africa, from logistical complexities to cultural nuances and the need for reliable local partnerships, are significant but not insurmountable. By viewing these challenges as opportunities for innovation, deeper engagement, and collaboration, mentorship programs can evolve to become more effective, inclusive, and impactful. Through strategic planning, the adoption of technology, and a commitment to cultural exchange and understanding, the diaspora can navigate these hurdles to forge meaningful mentorship relationships that contribute to the empowerment of Africa's youth and the broader development of the continent.

The exploration of the African diaspora's role in mentorship underscores a narrative of hope, resilience, and transformative potential. Through the lens of this chapter, it becomes evident that the diaspora's engagement in mentorship is not just a contribution but a cornerstone in shaping the future of Africa. Their unique position as bridges between worlds—carrying the richness of African heritage and the breadth of global experiences—enables them to impart invaluable knowledge, skills, and perspectives that are critical to the continent's development.

Challenges such as logistical hurdles, cultural nuances, and the quest for reliable local partnerships, while significant, also present opportunities for innovation and deeper connection. These obstacles, navigated with creativity and commitment, pave the way for mentorship models that are both impactful and sustainable. The diaspora's capacity to leverage technology, foster cross-cultural understanding, and build robust networks offers a blueprint for mentorship that transcends borders and barriers.

As we conclude this exploration of the African diaspora's role in mentorship, the path forward calls for a strategic harnessing of this vast potential. The integration of diaspora expertise and resources into mentorship initiatives requires not only the commitment of the diaspora itself but also the collaborative effort of local communities, governments, and international organizations. Together, these stakeholders can create an ecosystem of mentorship that is rich in diversity, innovation, and impact.

The vision of an equitable, prosperous, and innovative Africa is within reach, with mentorship serving as a key driver. The diaspora's continued investment in and expansion of mentorship initiatives are crucial steps toward this vision. By embracing the challenges as opportunities for growth and leveraging the unique strengths of the diaspora, mentorship can continue to be a powerful tool for personal development, community empowerment, and societal transformation.

In harnessing the untapped potential of the African diaspora in mentorship, we unlock the door to a future where every African youth has the guidance, support, and opportunities needed to thrive. The role of the African diaspora in mentorship is not just significant; it is essential. As we move forward, let us do so with a renewed commitment to collaboration, innovation, and the belief that together, we can shape a brighter future for Africa.

The future of mentorship lies in the ability to weave the rich tapestry of the diaspora's global experiences with the vibrant potential of Africa's youth. This interconnectedness fosters a mentorship culture that transcends geographical boundaries and cultural differences, making it possible for young Africans to benefit from a diverse range of knowledge and skills. By creating supportive networks and leveraging digital platforms, we can ensure that mentorship remains a dynamic and inclusive force for good.

Embracing this collaborative approach, stakeholders can foster environments where mentorship initiatives flourish, driving forward the socio-economic development of the continent. The diaspora's engagement brings invaluable perspectives and resources that, when combined with local efforts, can lead to groundbreaking advancements and opportunities. It is through this synergy that mentorship can truly transform lives and communities, paving the way for sustainable growth and development across Africa.

As we envision the road ahead, it is clear that the potential of the African diaspora in mentorship is boundless. The commitment to nurturing the next generation of leaders, innovators, and change-makers is a testament to the enduring connection between the diaspora and their home countries. Together, we can build a legacy of mentorship that not only uplifts individuals but also contributes to the broader goal of a thriving, self-sufficient Africa. Let us move forward with a collective spirit of determination and optimism, knowing that through mentorship, we hold the power to shape a future full of promise and possibility.

IMPLEMENTING EFFECTIVE MENTORSHIP PROGRAMS

In the dynamic world of mentorship, successfully launching and sustaining programs that genuinely benefit young Africans involves much more than initial enthusiasm—it requires strategic execution grounded in thorough planning and ongoing evaluation. This chapter explores the essential steps necessary for developing effective mentorship initiatives that can have a lasting impact on the lives of participants and contribute positively to broader societal development.

The process begins with a comprehensive understanding of the target demographic's needs and aspirations, which is crucial for crafting programs that are both relevant and impactful. By engaging directly with potential mentees, organizers can gain insights into the specific challenges and opportunities that these programs should address. This foundational step ensures that the mentorship provided is not only tailored to the actual needs of the youth but also enhances their personal and professional growth in meaningful ways.

Setting clear, measurable objectives from the start is another critical component. These objectives not only guide the program's development but also serve as benchmarks for later evaluation. They help stakeholders understand what success looks like and how it can be quantified, which is essential for securing ongoing support from funders and maintaining the program's focus.

The initial launch, while a significant milestone, marks the beginning of the mentorship journey rather than its culmination. Effective mentorship programs require robust mechanisms for continuous evaluation and feedback. This adaptive approach ensures that programs remain responsive to the evolving needs of mentees and can pivot accordingly to address new challenges as they arise. Regular assessments allow program managers to refine and improve their strategies, ensuring that the mentorship remains effective and relevant over time.

Implementing successful mentorship programs also involves navigating various challenges, including resource allocation, stakeholder engagement, and logistical hurdles. These can be overcome by fostering strong partnerships with local communities, NGOs, educational institutions, and even the private sector. Such collaborations can enhance the resource base, expand the program's reach, and infuse it with a diverse range of perspectives and expertise.

Ultimately, this chapter aims to provide readers with practical insights and strategies for implementing mentorship initiatives that are not just operational but also sustainable and impactful. By focusing on careful planning, execution, and continuous improvement, stakeholders can create mentorship programs that empower young Africans and contribute significantly to the socio-economic development of the continent.

Needs Assessment And Program Design

Creating an effective mentorship program begins not with a blueprint but with listening—a deep, involved process of understanding the unique challenges and dreams of the community it aims to serve. This isn't just about rolling out a well-intentioned program; it's about making sure it's the right program for the specific needs and aspirations of its participants, especially the vibrant youth of Africa.

The journey starts with a thorough needs assessment. This means not just surveys or scattered conversations, but a series of structured engagements—focus groups, interviews, and community meetings that reach into the heart of the target demographic. It's about tapping into the community's pulse, discovering what young people, their families, educators, and local leaders truly need and expect from such an initiative. For instance, in a community grappling with high youth unemployment, the focus might shift naturally towards vocational training and career guidance. In contrast, a region struggling with educational attainment might benefit more from academic support and resources that enhance learning opportunities.

From these rich, ground-level insights, setting clear, measurable, and achievable objectives becomes possible. These objectives aren't just lofty ideals; they are practical, actionable targets that guide every aspect of the program's development and execution. They ensure that every strategic decision—from curriculum design to mentor recruitment—aligns with the identified needs, enhancing the program's relevance and impact.

Designing the program is the next critical step. Here, the question of 'how' comes into play—how to structure the mentorship, how to match mentors with mentees, and whether to conduct sessions face-to-face or online. This phase also involves determining the resources required, which can range from funding and personnel to materials and facilities. It's also the perfect stage to forge partnerships with local businesses, educational institutions, and perhaps even governmental bodies, each bringing unique strengths and resources to the table.

Engaging potential mentors and mentees in this design phase is crucial. Their input can refine the program, tailoring activities to be more effective and ensuring the communication methods resonate with the participants. This collaborative approach doesn't just enhance the program's design; it builds a sense of ownership and commitment among everyone involved.

Setting this strong foundation is pivotal. It ensures that the mentorship program, once launched, is not just another initiative but a transformative force capable of truly making a difference in the lives of young Africans. It's about crafting a program that not only meets immediate needs but also fosters long-term personal and community development—creating a nurturing ground for young leaders who are as resilient as they are visionary. This thoughtful, thorough early planning is what allows mentorship programs to thrive, adapting and growing over time to meet new challenges and reach new heights.

Recruitment Of Mentors And Mentees

The recruitment of mentors and mentees stands as a critical phase in the lifecycle of mentorship programs, dictating not only the immediate effectiveness of the initiative but also its long-term sustainability and impact. The process requires a strategic approach, ensuring that selected mentors possess the necessary qualities to guide and support mentees, and that mentees are those who stand to gain significantly from the program. This dual approach ensures a fruitful mentorship experience for all parties involved.

Selecting mentors for mentorship programs is a comprehensive process that ensures mentors not only have the necessary expertise and experience but also demonstrate a deep commitment to their roles and an ability to connect effectively with mentees. Mentors must bring significant knowledge and relevant experiences to provide practical insights in areas such as academic, professional, or personal development. For example, a mentor in a business mentorship program should have a substantial background in business management or entrepreneurship to offer actionable advice.

A genuine commitment to mentoring is crucial, which goes beyond the willingness to spend time with mentees. It involves a desire to see others grow and succeed, often evaluated through interviews or motivational letters where potential mentors express their intentions and goals within the program.

The ability to relate to mentees on a personal level, offering empathy and understanding, is also essential. Effective mentors can communicate at the mentee's level, respect cultural differences, and provide support in ways that resonate with the mentee. This capability is often derived from mentors' own experiences that mirror those of the mentees or from their ability to empathize with diverse life experiences.

Training and preparation are also critical as not all mentors possess the necessary skills for effective mentoring from the start. Programs often provide training covering communication skills, boundary setting, and specific mentoring techniques relevant to the program's focus. A mentor's willingness to participate in such training is a significant indicator of their dedication and professionalism.

The recruitment process includes detailed applications, thorough interviews, and background checks to assess each candidate's suitability. This process ensures that individuals selected as mentors are knowledgeable and possess the right motives and interpersonal skills to impact mentees positively.

Overall, the mentor selection process is vital for the success of mentorship programs, ensuring mentors are well-equipped to handle various situations and can significantly impact mentees' personal and professional development. This process supports the overarching goal of mentorship: to facilitate meaningful development and growth.

Recruiting mentees who will benefit the most from mentorship programs involves a strategic approach that combines effective outreach and a commitment to inclusivity. By ensuring the program is accessible to all, regardless of background or circumstances, it enriches the mentorship experience with diverse perspectives and insights.

Targeted outreach is essential, utilizing schools, community organizations, social media, and other platforms to connect with potential mentees. These efforts should clearly communicate the benefits of the program, what it entails, and the criteria for participation. For example, a mentorship program might partner with local schools to conduct workshops that introduce students to the opportunities available through mentorship, highlighting how it can support their academic and personal growth.

Inclusivity and accessibility are cornerstones of effective mentorship programs. Eliminating barriers to participation—whether they are logistical, financial, or cultural—is crucial. This might involve providing transportation for mentees, offering programs at no cost, or ensuring that materials are available in multiple languages to accommodate non-native speakers.

Engagement and motivation are also key to attracting mentees. This can be achieved by showcasing success stories from alumni of the mentorship program, offering incentives like scholarships or access to exclusive workshops, and demonstrating the tangible benefits of participation, such as improved career prospects and personal development.

The matching process is a critical component once mentees are recruited. Effective matching involves pairing mentors and mentees based on shared interests, goals, and backgrounds to foster a productive and supportive relationship. This process might include detailed questionnaires that gather information about each mentee's interests and career aspirations, as well as each mentor's strengths and experiences, ensuring alignments that enhance the mentoring experience.

Through these strategic approaches, mentorship programs can successfully recruit and retain mentees who are most likely to benefit from and contribute to the mentorship experience, laying a strong foundation for impactful relationships that support personal development, community engagement, and societal progress.

Mentor and mentee recruitment, when done thoughtfully and strategically, can transform mentorship programs into powerful engines of personal and professional growth. It ensures that mentors are well-equipped and committed, while mentees are motivated and prepared to engage fully, making the entire process rewarding and effective. This thoughtful approach to recruitment not only builds strong, supportive relationships but also paves the way for lasting positive impact on individuals and communities alike.

Training And Support

Understanding the profound impact of a well-structured mentorship program hinges not just on launching it with enthusiasm but also on backing it up with solid training and support structures. These elements are not just peripheral extras; they are central cogs that ensure the mentorship engine runs smoothly, creating an environment where both mentors and mentees thrive and extract the maximum benefit from their interactions.

Training for both mentors and mentees is the launching pad for this. It's not just about equipping mentors with the basics of the program's goals or teaching them how to navigate the mentoring relationship with professionalism and empathy. It's also about setting a stage where mentors understand their profound role in shaping mentees' lives, not through authority, but through guidance, support, and advocacy. This involves detailed sessions on communication skills where the art of active listening is just as important as the ability to give advice. Mentors learn to provide feedback that's constructive rather than critical, fostering a growth mindset rather than a fixed one.

Mentees, on their part, aren't just passive recipients in this learning process. Orientation sessions help them grasp the structure and deeper goals of the mentorship, setting clear expectations on what they can gain and how they can actively engage in their own growth process. It's about empowering them to set realistic goals and encouraging them to take initiative, which transforms the mentorship from a simple guidance program to a personal development journey.

But the true test of a mentorship program's mettle isn't in the launching but in its sustained flight. This is where ongoing support plays a crucial role. Regular check-ins are vital, acting as touchpoints that help both mentors and mentees feel continuously supported and valued. These aren't just bureaucratic tick-box exercises; they are opportunities to recalibrate and align the mentorship journey to the mentee's evolving needs and circumstances.

Furthermore, supplementing the core mentorship with additional learning resources—be it articles, books, or specialized workshops—enriches the experience, keeping it vibrant and relevant. This is complemented by peer support groups which offer communal spaces for mentors and mentees to exchange ideas and challenges, adding a layer of communal learning to the individualized mentorship.

Professional development opportunities for mentors, and practical exposure for mentees, such as internships and job shadowing, bridge the gap between theory and practice. These opportunities not only enhance skills but also embed the mentorship teachings in real-world contexts, making the learning profound and applicable.

Feedback mechanisms are the final piece of this comprehensive support system. They allow for a two-way communication channel where the impact of the program can be evaluated and improved continuously. By embracing a culture of feedback, mentorship programs can stay dynamic and responsive, evolving with the needs of their participants and the demands of the wider environment.

In sum, the real power of mentorship programs lies not just in matching mentors with mentees but in how these relationships are nurtured over time through thoughtful training and robust support systems. This ensures that mentorship is more than just a passing influence but a transformative experience that contributes significantly to individual growth and collective community development.

Monitoring And Evaluation

In the vast landscape of mentorship, ensuring a program not only launches but thrives over time, hinges on robust monitoring and evaluation (M&E). This isn't merely about ticking boxes or compiling data to please stakeholders. Rather, it's about deeply understanding the impact these programs have, refining them continually, and making sure they remain aligned with their foundational goals.

Evaluating a mentorship program is complex, requiring both the hard edges of quantitative data and the nuanced touch of qualitative feedback. We're looking at more than just numbers and outcomes here. We need to tap into the real-life experiences of participants, understand their journeys, and gauge the program's transformative power on their lives and careers. This dual approach ensures a rounded view, capturing not just what changes, but how and why these changes occur.

Feedback from participants, for instance, is gold dust. Through surveys, interviews, and focus groups, we get to hear what's resonating, what's missing, and how the experience molds their paths. It's about pinpointing what works and what needs tweaking, making sure the program is as responsive and impactful as possible.

Tracking mentee progress is another pillar in assessing impact. It's not just about where they end up but monitoring their journey—be it academic strides, skill acquisition, or professional development. This helps paint a picture of the mentorship's effectiveness, providing concrete evidence of how it's fostering growth.

And it's not just about measuring up to our expectations but stacking our outcomes against our initial objectives. Are we hitting our marks on increasing youth employment or boosting academic success? This isn't just about internal housekeeping. It's crucial for demonstrating the program's value to funders and stakeholders, showcasing its merits, and justifying continued or increased investment.

But true strength in a mentorship program lies in what happens after these assessments. It's about what we do with the insights gleaned. This is where adaptation and continuous improvement play starring roles. Using what we learn to refine and enhance the program ensures it stays relevant and effective amidst evolving needs and challenges. This could mean tweaking our methods, scaling successful strategies, or sometimes, overhauling aspects that aren't working.

Fostering a culture of continuous learning within the program itself is key. Engaging everyone involved—from mentors to mentees to stakeholders—in this cyclical feedback loop ensures that the program isn't just evolving based on theoretical data but is also grounded in the lived experiences and collective wisdom of its community.

Periodic reviews, regular updates, and strategic pivots based on ongoing M&E make the program dynamic—not just a static entity but a living, breathing ecosystem that adapts and grows. This isn't about change for change's sake but about intelligent evolution, driven by data and narratives that guide us toward more impactful interventions.

Moreover, the scalability and potential replication of successful elements hinge on solid M&E practices. Understanding what works and transplanting these successes into new settings can amplify the impact, allowing the benefits of proven mentorship models to reach broader audiences.

At its heart, effective M&E breathes life into mentorship programs. It transforms them from static models into vibrant, adaptive frameworks that not only meet the current needs of participants but are also poised to evolve with them. This ongoing cycle of assessment, adaptation, and improvement isn't just administrative —it's the pulse that ensures mentorship programs not only survive but thrive, making a lasting difference in the lives of young Africans and, by extension, the broader fabric of society. Through meticulous and thoughtful M&E, these initiatives can continue to be a beacon of development, empowerment, and change.

Sustainability And Growth

Diving into the world of mentorship, it's clear that the sustainability and growth of these programs are not just hopes but necessities if they are to continue making a lasting impact. For mentorship initiatives to thrive long-term and extend their reach, they require a robust foundation not only in passion but also in practical strategy.

When considering the financial health and longevity of a mentorship program, it's crucial to look beyond single funding sources. Diversification is key. This might involve tapping into a mix of grants, sponsorships, donations, and community fundraising events. Each of these streams comes with its own set of challenges and opportunities, but together, they create a financial safety net that can help sustain the program through ups and downs.

Strategic partnerships also play a critical role. Aligning with local businesses, educational institutions, and community organizations can do more than just bolster financial resources; these alliances can offer in-kind support like venues for mentorship sessions or donations of equipment and materials. The synergy from these collaborations not only enriches the program but also embeds it more deeply within the community, enhancing its relevance and impact.

Some mentorship programs might even explore social enterprise models where they create their own revenue streams. This could be through offering paid workshops, consulting services, or selling products that align with their mission. Such activities must carefully balance generating income with the primary goal of mentorship, ensuring one does not undermine the other.

As programs prove their effectiveness and establish a track record of success, scaling becomes a realistic ambition. However, expansion isn't just about casting a wider net—it's about replicating success in a way that maintains program quality and stays true to core objectives. This might involve adapting the program to meet the specific cultural and social needs of new communities, which requires careful planning and local engagement.

Using technology can facilitate this growth, allowing programs to reach wider audiences while maintaining personal connections. Online platforms and digital tools can bridge geographical divides, bringing mentorship to remote or underserved areas and providing scalable solutions that support a growing mentee base.

Lastly, as a program grows, so too must its internal capacities. This involves training new staff, scaling up operations, and enhancing monitoring and evaluation processes to ensure that as the scope of the program expands, its quality and effectiveness remain high.

The cornerstone of utilizing mentorship as a tool for social change in Africa lies in the implementation of effective mentorship programs. This foundational element is crucial; without it, the potential for social change through mentorship remains unrealized. It's within this context that I believe SAYes Youth Mentoring stands out as one of Africa's premier mentorship programs. My journey with SAYes began as a mentee in 2012, and I witnessed a remarkable transformation when Dr. Andrew Dellis took over as Operational Director in 2015. I observed firsthand the complete overhaul of the program, to the extent that I'd confidently assert the program was redesigned under his leadership.

Dr. Dellis embarked on a comprehensive assessment and redesign of the program, laying down a clear roadmap for the recruitment of mentors and mentees. He introduced robust training and support materials, focusing particularly on preparing both mentors and mentees effectively. One of the significant shifts was the initiation of an annual Monitoring and Evaluation process, aimed at driving growth and ensuring sustainability. As a result of these strategic enhancements, the program has not only expanded across South Africa but has also achieved international reach. This experience underscored for me the critical importance of implementing effective mentorship programs.

Through these developments, SAYes has demonstrated the power of a well-structured mentorship program in providing meaningful guidance and support to young individuals. The organization's success story serves as a valuable model for the design and execution of mentorship initiatives, highlighting the impact such programs can have on personal development and broader societal change.

In wrapping up this exploration of effective mentorship programs, we see the profound transformative power they hold for Africa's youth. The journey to impactful mentorship demands meticulous planning, diligent execution, and thoughtful management, each a cornerstone to guiding young individuals toward their personal and professional goals. This endeavor requires not just adherence to the principles of mentorship but also a commitment to a culture of excellence, innovation, and adaptability.

Through the pages of this chapter, it's been emphasized that the success of mentorship programs depends heavily on understanding the specific needs of the community, establishing clear and attainable goals, carefully selecting and training mentors and mentees, and continuously providing support and resources. Moreover, robust monitoring and evaluation practices are vital, ensuring that programs remain aligned with their objectives and responsive to the evolving needs of participants.

The call to action for all stakeholders—governments, NGOs, the private sector, and educational institutions—is clear: mentorship is an essential tool for cultivating the continent's future leaders, innovators, and changemakers. By fostering an environment of collaboration, securing sustainable funding, and remaining receptive to lessons learned from ongoing evaluations, mentorship initiatives can achieve growth and adaptability.

Conclusively, the deployment of effective mentorship programs is a strategic investment in the future of Africa's youth and, by extension, the continent itself. With sustained effort, a commitment to quality, and a responsive approach to the ever-changing mentorship landscape, these programs can persist as vital platforms for personal growth, professional development, and societal progress across Africa.

EVALUATING THE IMPACT OF MENTORSHIP PROGRAMS

The evaluation of mentorship programs transcends mere administrative oversight; it is a vital component in understanding their true value and impact. In the realm of development and empowerment, the success of these programs cannot solely be quantified by immediate results. Instead, a more nuanced approach is required, one that considers the profound and often gradual transformation experienced by individuals and, by extension, their communities. This chapter aims to explore the multifaceted nature of evaluating mentorship programs, shedding light on the methodologies that enable a comprehensive assessment of their outcomes and the significance of gauging their long-term effects.

Evaluating the impact of mentorship involves a blend of quantitative and qualitative measures, each offering insights into different dimensions of effectiveness. From the advancement in mentees' academic performance and professional achievements to the subtler shifts in their confidence levels, social skills, and personal growth, the metrics of success are diverse. Moreover, the broader societal implications of mentorship, such as its contribution to reducing youth unemployment, fostering social cohesion, and promoting gender equality, add layers of complexity to the evaluation process.

This chapter will navigate through the various approaches used to assess mentorship programs, highlighting the challenges and opportunities inherent in capturing their true essence. Understanding the long-term effects of these initiatives is crucial, not just for validating their worth but also for informing future strategies and interventions. Through a detailed examination of evaluation methodologies, this section aims to equip stakeholders with the knowledge and tools necessary to discern and enhance the enduring impact of mentorship programs on individuals and communities across Africa.

Metrics And Methodologies

Evaluating the impact of mentorship programs goes beyond mere numbers; it's about understanding the transformative journey of individuals and communities. From my perspective, combining both quantitative and qualitative approaches is essential for capturing the true essence of these impacts. Let me delve deeper into this.

Quantitative metrics are foundational—they give us a solid, measurable grasp of a program's scale and immediate outcomes. For example, by tracking the number of participants, we can gauge a program's reach. Academic improvements and post-program employment rates offer concrete evidence of the program's effectiveness. These figures help validate the mentorship's role in enhancing educational achievements and job readiness.

But the story doesn't end with numbers. Qualitative data brings the human experience into focus, providing depth that numbers alone cannot. It's through stories, testimonials, and detailed case studies that we really grasp how mentorship transforms lives. Interviews and focus groups are invaluable here, revealing subtle shifts in mentees' attitudes, confidence, and aspirations—nuances that might be invisible in quantitative data alone.

Combining these metrics gives us a holistic view. Quantitative data can show us trends and patterns, helping to identify which parts of a program are working well, while qualitative insights can explain why certain aspects are effective, or how they might be improved. For instance, if quantitative data shows an improvement in academic performance, qualitative feedback from mentees might reveal that this success is due to increased self-confidence or better study techniques shared by mentors.

Implementing this dual approach requires careful planning. From setting up initial data collection to ensure there's a baseline for comparison, to engaging with program participants throughout their journey, every step is critical. The aim is to ensure that mentorship programs are not just effective but also adaptable to the evolving needs of mentees and the wider community.

Ultimately, the blend of quantitative and qualitative metrics not only validates the effectiveness of mentorship programs but also enriches our understanding of their broader impact. This comprehensive approach ensures that mentorship programs can continue to evolve, underpinned by a commitment to real-world effectiveness and continuous improvement. Through this detailed evaluation, mentorship programs can prove to be powerful catalysts for personal growth and community development.

Methodologies For Effective Evaluation

Evaluating the impact of mentorship programs is a complex task that demands a nuanced approach, blending different research methodologies to capture the full spectrum of a program's influence on its participants. In my view, the integration of mixed methods, longitudinal studies, and comparative analysis forms the cornerstone of a robust evaluation framework that can offer valuable insights into both the tangible and intangible outcomes of mentorship.

The mixed-methods approach is crucial because it allows for a comprehensive analysis that combines hard data with human stories. For instance, while quantitative metrics might highlight an uptick in academic performance or employment rates among mentees, qualitative data gathered through interviews or testimonials can provide deeper insight into how these changes impact mentees' lives. Such qualitative data often reveal increased confidence, improved interpersonal relationships, or a greater sense of purpose, which are just as significant as any statistical improvement but far harder to quantify.

Longitudinal studies are invaluable for understanding the enduring effects of mentorship. The true value of mentorship might not be fully realized in the short term. These studies, which track participants over several years, help in assessing whether the positive impacts observed during or immediately after the program sustain over time, such as career progression, continuous personal development, or long-term contributions to the community. They also help identify whether any initial improvements wane, suggesting areas where ongoing support might be necessary.

Comparative analysis, by comparing participants in mentorship programs with a control group who did not receive such mentoring, evaluators can isolate the effects of the mentorship from other variables. This approach is particularly potent in illustrating the unique benefits of mentorship, demonstrating its efficacy in promoting better outcomes in various domains, be it academic, professional, or personal.

Implementing these methodologies effectively involves meticulous planning to ensure that data collection tools are well-designed and that the research is carried out ethically. This means designing surveys that accurately capture necessary information, ensuring informed consent is obtained from all participants, and maintaining strict confidentiality protocols. Furthermore, the ethical implications of such studies are paramount. Researchers must navigate these sensitively, ensuring that participants are not only informed of the purpose of the research but are also assured of their privacy and the confidentiality of their responses.

Through these comprehensive evaluation methodologies, stakeholders—from program designers to funders—can gain a clearer picture of what aspects of mentorship work, what needs improvement, and how mentorship is fostering change. This understanding is crucial for refining existing programs and designing new ones that are more effective, thereby maximizing the impact of mentorship initiatives across diverse communities. This thoughtful, systematic approach to evaluation underscores the commitment to not just conducting mentorship programs but to continually enhancing them, ensuring they deliver the maximum possible benefit to all involved.

By embracing these robust evaluation methodologies, mentorship programs can be more transparent and accountable, demonstrating their true value to all stakeholders. This approach ultimately contributes to the credibility and sustainability of mentorship initiatives, ensuring that they continue to evolve and meet the needs of the communities they serve. It also highlights the importance of not only focusing on immediate outcomes but also considering the long-term effects and potential of mentorship, paving the way for more impactful and enduring programs.

Assessing Outcomes And Long-Term Effects

Evaluating the outcomes and the long-term effects of mentorship programs is crucial for understanding their real-world impact. This process not only highlights immediate successes but also sheds light on the deeper, enduring transformations that mentorship can instigate both for individuals and their communities. Such thorough evaluation is vital not just for the fine-tuning of these programs but also for validating the investments made and showcasing their value to those who fund and support them.

The most visible and straightforward outcomes to measure are often the immediate ones. For example, if a mentorship program focuses on academic enhancement, one clear metric of its success would be an improvement in the mentees' grades. Such tangible results offer proof of the program's effectiveness in elevating academic engagement and performance right after its conclusion. Similarly, mentorship can significantly bolster social skills like communication and teamwork, essential for both personal growth and professional success. Assessing these skills right after program completion provides immediate evidence of the mentorship's impact.

For career-focused mentorship, immediate outcomes might also include better preparedness for the job market, more defined career goals, and enhanced job-related skills. These can be measured through surveys or interviews conducted as the program wraps up, helping to gauge how ready mentees feel to tackle their professional journeys.

However, the true test of a mentorship program often lies in its long-term effects, which can be more challenging to measure but are incredibly revealing. Tracking career advancement over several years can show how mentorship has facilitated professional growth, promotions, and other significant milestones. Moreover, the long-term evaluation might focus on leadership development, assessing whether mentees take on leadership roles and how effectively they contribute to their organizations and communities.

Perhaps one of the most profound long-term effects is the proliferation of a mentorship culture within communities. This can often be observed when former mentees step into mentoring roles themselves, perpetuating a cycle of guidance and support. To effectively measure this, ongoing engagement with program alumni is necessary, which could involve regular follow-ups, the establishment of alumni networks, and continuous monitoring of their mentorship activities.

Implementing such comprehensive evaluation strategies involves a commitment to longitudinal studies and consistent data gathering. This may include repeated surveys, structured interviews, and maintaining active communication channels that keep alumni connected to the program. These efforts help not only in assessing the long-term impacts but also in maintaining a strong, supportive community around the mentorship program, enhancing both its sustainability and its depth of impact.

By adopting a meticulous approach to both immediate and long-term evaluations, mentorship programs can continuously evolve to meet the changing needs of participants and the broader community goals. This ongoing assessment process underscores the transformative potential of mentorship, highlighting its importance as a tool for personal development, professional growth, and community enrichment. In embracing both quantitative and qualitative metrics, and by committing to the long haul of tracking and support, mentorship initiatives can maximize their effectiveness, ensuring they deliver substantial, enduring benefits to individuals and their communities.

Challenges In Evaluation

Evaluating the impact of mentorship programs isn't just a box-checking exercise; it's a deep dive into understanding their effectiveness and refining their approaches for better future outcomes. This process is vital, not only for confirming the value of these programs but also for steering their ongoing improvements and securing necessary funding. But the path to insightful evaluation is fraught with hurdles, requiring a nuanced approach to genuinely capture the influence of mentorship on both individuals and their communities.

Immediate outcomes of mentorship are typically the most straightforward to measure. These can range from noticeable improvements in a mentee's academic records to enhancements in their social skills and readiness for the workplace. These metrics provide a quick snapshot of effectiveness right after program completion. We rely on tools like surveys and direct feedback from everyone involved—mentors, mentees, and sometimes educators or employers—to gather this data. These insights are crucial for on-the-fly adjustments that keep the mentorship relevant and impactful.

However, the true essence of mentorship often lies in its long-term effects, which can be far more challenging to assess but are equally important. We're looking to see if mentorship has fostered significant professional growth, leadership qualities, and perhaps most importantly, a sustained culture of mentoring itself, where former mentees become mentors. This continuation of mentorship culture is a beautiful outcome, symbolizing a self-sustaining cycle of empowerment.

Yet, evaluating these long-term impacts comes with its own set of challenges:

Attribution: One of the main difficulties here is directly linking improvements in a mentee's life to the mentorship they received, amidst all other variables in their environment. To address this, control groups or comparative studies are often employed, allowing us to isolate the effects of the mentorship from other factors.

Engagement: Maintaining contact with program alumni to track these long-term changes is another hurdle. People move on, become busy with their lives and careers, and may disengage from the program networks. Building an alumni network that offers real value to its members—through networking opportunities, professional development, and continuous learning—can help keep them engaged. This not only aids in maintaining contact but also ensures a rich reservoir of data for ongoing evaluation.

Navigating these challenges requires careful program design and a commitment to innovative evaluation methodologies. By keeping our alumni engaged and using robust methods to isolate the effects of our programs, we can truly understand and showcase the value of mentorship. Effective evaluation is key to demonstrating that mentorship is not just a feel-good initiative but a potent tool for personal development and broader community improvement. Through meticulous and thoughtful assessment, mentorship programs can continue to refine their strategies and expand their impact, helping to shape a more capable, empowered future generation.

As we reflect on our journey through the world of mentorship programs, it becomes evident just how crucial the evaluation phase is. This isn't just a formality but a fundamental part of confirming the value and effectiveness of mentorship efforts. It's about more than just assessing; it's about deeply understanding the impact these programs have—both immediately and over the long haul.

Evaluating these programs thoroughly means employing a range of methods to truly see the effects. We're talking about a mix of immediate feedback like enhanced academic performance or better social skills, and long-term benefits such as career growth and the cultivation of new mentors from program alumni. These insights don't just highlight successes; they help pinpoint where improvements are needed, ensuring that mentorship remains relevant and responsive.

Carrying out such comprehensive evaluations is no small feat. It requires a thoughtful selection of both quantitative measures (like test scores or employment rates) and qualitative feedback (like personal stories or participant interviews). These metrics give us a full picture, showing not just the outcomes but the transformations participants experience.

The commitment to this rigorous evaluation process reflects a deeper dedication to making mentorship work effectively. It's about proving that these programs do more than just occupy time; they change lives. By consistently refining these programs based on solid data and genuine feedback, stakeholders can ensure that mentorship remains a potent tool for growth and positive change.

When we implement mentorship programs effectively and back them up with robust evaluations, we lay a solid foundation for not just meeting but exceeding the developmental goals of individuals and communities alike. This commitment to continuous improvement and real impact drives the success of mentorship programs and cements their role in fostering societal progress.

The true essence of mentorship lies in its ability to transform lives and build stronger communities. By embracing comprehensive evaluation methods, we ensure that every mentorship initiative not only achieves its goals but also adapts to the evolving needs of its participants. This holistic approach to evaluation is what makes mentorship a sustainable and impactful force for positive change. Through dedication, thorough analysis, and a relentless pursuit of excellence, mentorship programs can continue to empower individuals and contribute significantly to the broader tapestry of societal advancement.

APPROACHES TO MENTORSHIP IN AFRICA

In the dynamic realm of African mentorship, the shift towards innovative approaches reflects the continent's resilience and inventive spirit. Africa's diverse challenges—its vast geography, rich cultural tapestry, and varied resource availability—are being met with groundbreaking mentorship models that enhance accessibility, impact, and reach.

One of the most transformative trends is the rise of digital platforms. Technology has become a cornerstone for mentorship, enabling connections that transcend physical and geographical limitations. Through online programs, virtual workshops, and mobile applications, mentors and mentees can forge impactful relationships from afar. This digital approach democratizes access to mentorship, ensuring that opportunities are not limited by location, thereby fostering equitable growth and learning.

Community-based initiatives represent another innovative stride, leveraging the inherent strength of local networks. These programs integrate the cultural and communal wisdom of African societies, grounding mentorship in familiar customs and values. By tapping into local traditions and community dynamics, these initiatives ensure that mentorship is not only culturally resonant but also sustains and supports the communal fabric, making it a powerful tool for grassroots development.

Cross-cultural international partnerships expand the scope of mentorship further, introducing African mentees and mentors to global perspectives and networks. Collaborations with entities outside Africa enrich the mentorship experience, offering access to a broader range of resources, knowledge, and opportunities. These partnerships not only facilitate a cultural exchange but also help in knitting a global support network that enhances the mentors' and mentees' exposure to international standards and practices.

These innovative approaches underscore a broader narrative: Africa is not merely catching up with global trends in mentorship but is actively shaping them to fit its unique context. By embracing technology, community, and international cooperation, Africa is setting the stage for a mentorship model that is both locally grounded and globally connected. This progressive outlook ensures that mentorship remains a pivotal force in nurturing the continent's future leaders, innovators, and change-makers, steering Africa towards sustained growth and development.

Digital Mentorship Platforms

Digital mentorship platforms are revolutionizing the way mentorship is accessed and utilized across Africa, representing a significant leap in how support and guidance are delivered. These platforms harness technology to broaden the scope of mentorship, overcoming geographical limitations, and enhancing both the flexibility and scalability of these programs, which is crucial in a continent as vast and varied as Africa.

One of the standout features of digital platforms is their ability to make mentorship accessible to anyone with internet access. This is particularly transformative in regions where physical distances and insufficient infrastructure often limit opportunities for growth and professional development. With digital platforms, young people in even the most remote areas can tap into networks of expertise and support that were previously out of reach, effectively democratizing the learning and mentorship process.

The flexibility offered by these platforms also cannot be overstated. Traditional mentorship often demands synchronous communication and meetings, which can be challenging across different time zones or busy schedules. Digital platforms, however, allow for asynchronous interactions, enabling mentors and mentees to engage with each other at the most convenient times. This aspect ensures that individuals can balance their mentorship activities with personal and professional responsibilities, making the mentorship more adaptable and inclusive.

Scalability is another critical advantage. Digital platforms can support a large number of mentor-mentee pairs without a corresponding increase in administrative costs or resources. This scalability is essential for expanding the reach of mentorship initiatives, allowing them to impact a broader audience without necessitating significant infrastructural expansions.

A prime example of the power of these platforms is MENTORx, a pioneering app designed to connect young African entrepreneurs with seasoned business leaders worldwide. This platform tailors the mentorship experience, matching entrepreneurs with mentors who can provide sector-specific advice, strategic guidance, and global market insights. MENTORx facilitates not just knowledge exchange but also strategic networking, helping mentees to expand their professional connections and gain practical insights into navigating business challenges.

MENTORx particularly excels by providing structured mentorship through features like goal setting, progress tracking, and resource sharing, which enhance the mentorship experience and ensure that it delivers measurable benefits to the participants. Its success demonstrates how digital platforms can transcend traditional barriers, offering young African entrepreneurs' critical resources that propel their personal and professional growth.

Overall, digital mentorship platforms like MENTORx illustrate the transformative potential of technology in mentorship. They not only streamline the mentorship process but also create an expansive network of learning and development across Africa. As technology continues to advance, the scope and impact of digital mentorship are expected to grow, ushering in a new era of empowerment for Africa's youth, catalyzing their development, and by extension, that of their communities and the broader continent.

Community-Based Mentorship

Community-based mentorship is a transformative force within Africa, deeply rooted in the continent's rich communal traditions where mentorship is not just a formal program but a part of everyday life. This form of mentorship leverages local customs and knowledge, making it uniquely powerful and significantly relevant to the participants' cultural and communal realities.

At the heart of community-based mentorship are the local leaders, revered within their communities for their wisdom and experience. These leaders serve as mentors, lending authenticity and depth to the mentorship process. Their understanding of the local context ensures that the guidance provided is not only practical but deeply resonant with the cultural dynamics and societal norms of the community. This kind of mentorship isn't merely about professional development but about nurturing young individuals to thrive within their own cultural and societal frameworks.

Cultural relevance is crucial in these initiatives. Mentorship programs that succeed are those that integrate seamlessly with the local values and traditions, making them more than just an educational or professional resource—they become a part of the community's identity. This alignment with cultural values ensures that mentorship is perceived as a valuable and relevant tool for personal growth, accepted and embraced by all community members.

The empowerment that comes from community-based mentorship is profound. It involves active participation from all members of the community, with individuals often taking on dual roles as mentors and mentees over time. This reciprocal relationship not only enhances personal growth but also strengthens communal bonds. Over time, as mentees transition into mentor roles, they perpetuate a cycle of empowerment and development, ensuring the sustainability of the mentorship impact.

One poignant example is the Village Mentors program, which operates in rural areas across the continent. This initiative connects the youth with elders, facilitating the transfer of traditional skills and wisdom. It's a celebration of indigenous knowledge with the elders acting as custodians of the community's heritage while also equipping the youth with necessary modern skills. This program effectively demonstrates the seamless integration of traditional wisdom with contemporary needs, helping young people forge a strong sense of identity and community connection.

Through these programs, mentorship becomes a powerful tool for development—not just for individuals but for entire communities. The approach ensures that mentorship in Africa is not seen as an external imposition but as an organic, integral part of community life. As these initiatives continue to grow, they promise to nurture a generation that is not only well-equipped to handle the future's challenges but also deeply connected to their roots and cultural heritage. This blend of the old and the new, the traditional and the modern, is what makes community-based mentorship in Africa a true beacon of hope and transformation.

Cross-Cultural And International Mentorship

Cross-cultural and international mentorship has truly revolutionized the way mentorship programs are structured, broadening horizons, and fostering a deep, meaningful exchange between cultures. This innovative approach to mentorship transcends traditional geographic and cultural barriers, ushering in a new era of global interconnectedness that is indispensable for the next generation of African leaders. These programs not only enhance professional and personal development but also cultivate a profound understanding and appreciation of diverse cultural landscapes.

By integrating mentors from various cultural backgrounds and international experiences, these programs offer young Africans unparalleled insights into different ways of thinking and problem-solving. The diversity inherent in these relationships enriches the mentorship experience, pushing mentees to challenge their preconceptions and expand their worldviews. Imagine learning from a mentor who has navigated through multiple international markets or one who has led cross-cultural teams. Such experiences compel mentees to think more broadly, embracing innovative approaches to both old and new challenges.

Moreover, the international networks that mentees gain access to through these programs are invaluable. These aren't just contacts but are gateways to significant opportunities—be it in academia, career progression, or entrepreneurial ventures. For instance, a mentee might connect with someone during a session and find themselves working on a collaborative project across continents or even landing an internship in a completely different part of the world. These connections often evolve into long-term professional relationships and mentorships, providing continuous growth and learning opportunities.

Beyond the professional realm, the cultural exchange that unfolds within these mentorship frameworks enriches the mentees' personal growth. Engaging with a mentor from a different cultural background isn't just educational; it's a deep dive into a new set of traditions, ethics, and values. Such interactions enhance mentees' cultural sensitivity and equip them with the skills to navigate and succeed in a globalized world. They learn to communicate effectively across cultural boundaries, which is an invaluable skill in today's globally connected marketplace.

The benefits of cross-cultural and international mentorship extend beyond individual growth, impacting communities and industries by fostering a generation of well-rounded, globally minded leaders. These leaders are prepared not only to face global challenges but also to contribute uniquely African perspectives to global dialogs, enriching the international community's approach to solving complex global issues.

In essence, the shift towards incorporating diverse, cross-cultural, and international elements into mentorship programs represents a forward-thinking approach to education and professional development. It's about preparing young Africans not just for the jobs of today, but for participating actively and confidently in a world that is increasingly without borders. This dynamic, holistic approach to mentorship is what will cultivate the global citizens of tomorrow —individuals who are culturally astute, professionally skilled, and ready to make their mark on the world.

Case Study: Global Bridge Mentors

The Global Bridge Mentors program exemplifies the potential of cross-cultural and international mentorship to transform lives. This innovative initiative connects African students with mentors from around the world, enriching their educational and professional journeys with a wealth of diverse insights. The essence of this program lies in its ability to open doors to educational advancement and career development while fostering an environment rich in cultural exchange.

Through personalized one-on-one mentorship and interactive group sessions, students gain invaluable guidance on how to navigate their academic paths and leap into global opportunities. These experiences are tailored to prepare them for the demands of an increasingly interconnected world, equipping them with the skills necessary to thrive in international job markets.

What sets Global Bridge Mentors apart is its dual focus on professional development and cultural understanding. Participants engage in cross-cultural dialogues and collaborative projects that enhance their global citizenship, promoting mutual respect and understanding across different cultures. This aspect of the program is crucial; it transforms participants not only into skilled professionals but also into ambassadors of cultural exchange, ready to bridge divides and integrate diverse perspectives into their careers and daily lives.

The success of Global Bridge Mentors serves as a testament to the transformative power of extending mentorship beyond local and national confines. By embracing the richness of global diversity and fostering collaborative networks, such initiatives play a critical role in shaping individuals who are both professionally competent and culturally savvy.

As programs like Global Bridge Mentors continue to evolve, they highlight the immense benefits of incorporating global perspectives into mentorship. These programs pave the way for young Africans to emerge as leaders equipped to face global challenges, underscoring the importance of nurturing a generation that values and understands the importance of cultural diversity and global connectivity.

Exploring the innovative approaches to mentorship in Africa has unveiled a vibrant fusion where the power of tradition enhances modern innovation, where localized insights merge with global perspectives, and where technology serves as a bridge, connecting diverse learning experiences and developmental opportunities. This fascinating landscape is where digital platforms, revitalized community-based efforts, and cross-cultural as well as international partnerships showcase their dynamic and adaptive nature, playing a pivotal role in reshaping mentorship across the continent.

These progressive models do more than simply augment traditional mentorship; they are integral to its evolution, ensuring that mentorship in Africa remains pertinent and robust amidst global changes. The digital era, while presenting its unique challenges, also opens up extraordinary opportunities to broaden the scope and impact of mentorship. It makes these vital connections more accessible and inclusive than ever before.

Community-focused approaches continue to underscore the priceless value of local wisdom and collective growth, anchoring mentorship firmly within the rich cultural foundations from which it originated. Simultaneously, cross-cultural and international endeavors are not just opening doors but are also setting the stage for young Africans to become active shapers of the global landscape.

Looking forward, the ongoing innovation within mentorship practices holds tremendous promise not only to empower the youth of Africa but to propel them to new heights of personal success and leadership. The potential of these innovative methods to drive transformative change across the continent is vast. By supporting and fostering these developments, a diverse array of stakeholders —including governments, educators, community leaders, and international partners—can play a part in cultivating a mentorship ecosystem that is vibrant, diverse, and profoundly impactful.

The exploration of new methods in African mentorship paints a picture of a continent on the rise, one that is acutely aware of its challenges yet even more attuned to its enormous potential. As these initiatives continue to evolve and expand, they promise to unlock this potential, empowering Africa's youth to flourish in the 21st century and beyond, thereby crafting a future as rich and diverse as the continent itself.

VOICES FROM THE FIELD

Mentorship, as explored in this chapter, goes beyond traditional boundaries of guidance and learning, deeply embedding itself into the fabric of personal and professional growth. Through a collection of powerful testimonials from mentors and mentees, this chapter, "Voices from the Field," reveals the transformative impact of mentorship across Africa. Each story provides a vivid illustration of how mentorship has shaped individuals' lives and uplifted communities, offering a comprehensive view of its far-reaching effects.

Here, we delve into the essence of mentorship through the experiences of those who have lived it—mentees discovering their paths, mentors imparting wisdom, and communities witnessing extraordinary transformations. These narratives do more than just recount successes; they highlight the varied ways mentorship has catalyzed personal achievements and fostered enduring relationships.

From the transmission of traditional knowledge in rural villages to the molding of young entrepreneurs in bustling cities, these stories span the broad spectrum of mentorship's influence. They celebrate the triumphs and address the struggles, showcasing the resilience, determination, and spirit of collaboration that mentorship instills.

"Voices from the Field" invites readers on an inspirational journey through the compelling tales of individuals and communities across Africa, showcasing the significant, life-changing power of mentorship. It's a testament to how guided support and shared wisdom can shape futures and alter lives profoundly, highlighting the pivotal role mentorship plays in driving personal success and community development.

Transformations And Achievements

Mentorship serves as a beacon of hope and transformation, igniting the latent potential within individuals and communities across Africa. Through the lens of mentorship, numerous stories unfold, each narrating a journey of growth, resilience, and achievement. This section delves into the lives touched by mentorship, exploring the profound changes that have led to personal accomplishments and community betterment.

Individual Growth: mentorship has the unique capacity to foster significant personal and professional development. Take, for example, the story of Fatima, a young woman from a small village with dreams larger than her surroundings. Through mentorship, Fatima harnessed her passion for technology, transforming from a curious learner to an innovator. Her mentor, a seasoned tech entrepreneur, guided her through the complexities of launching a startup, providing both technical expertise and moral support. Today, Fatima's tech company addresses agricultural challenges in her community, showcasing the power of mentorship in turning potential into tangible achievement.

From Mentee to Leader: Aminata's story is a testament to the transformative power of mentorship. Initially a shy student with undirected ambition, Amina's engagement in a mentorship program was the turning point in her life. Her mentor, a public health professional, recognized Amina's passion for community wellness and guided her through the process of creating impactful health initiatives. Amina's leadership in establishing a community health project not only addressed pressing health issues but also positioned her as a respected leader. Her journey from uncertainty to influence exemplifies the profound impact mentorship can have on unlocking leadership potential and fostering community development.

Community Impact: beyond individual achievements, mentorship has the capacity to catalyze positive changes within communities. Stories abound of mentees who, inspired by their mentorship experiences, have initiated projects addressing local needs. For instance, Thomas, once a mentee in an environmental mentorship program, spearheaded a successful community recycling project, reducing waste and creating jobs. Such initiatives underscore the ripple effect of mentorship, where empowered individuals lead efforts that benefit their wider community.

Cross-Cultural Exchanges: mentorship programs that bridge cultural divides offer unique opportunities for growth and understanding.

Sarah, a participant in an international mentorship exchange, shares how her relationship with a mentor from a different cultural background expanded her worldview. The exchange allowed for rich discussions on global issues, fostering a deep appreciation for diversity and mutual respect. These cross-cultural mentorship experiences highlight the role of mentorship in promoting global citizenship and empathy.

Breaking Barriers: James's journey through mentorship illustrates its capacity to break down barriers and open up new horizons. Facing academic challenges and cultural obstacles, James was the first in his family to dream of higher education. His mentor, an academic advisor, provided not only academic support but also guidance on navigating the application process for university admission. James's subsequent acceptance into a prestigious university marked a significant milestone, demonstrating mentorship's critical role in educational attainment and the breaking of cycles of limitation.

The stories of Fatima, Aminata, Thomas, Sarah, and James are but a few examples of the remarkable transformations and achievements made possible by mentorship. Each narrative is a beacon, illuminating the path from potential to realization, from individual growth to community betterment, and from cultural awareness to barrier-breaking achievements. Mentorship in Africa is not just a tool for personal development; it is a catalyst for widespread change, inspiring a generation of leaders, innovators, and global citizens poised to shape the future.

Testimonials From Mentors

Mentorship, often perceived as a one-way street where knowledge and experience flow from mentor to mentee, is in reality a journey of mutual growth and discovery. The stories of mentors, rich with insights and reflections, reveal the profound impact that guiding others can have on their own lives. This section delves into the heart of the mentorship experience from the mentor's perspective, shedding light on the joys, challenges, and unexpected lessons that emerge from the mentor-mentee relationship.

Mentors often enter into mentorship with the intention of sharing their knowledge and supporting the next generation. However, as they navigate the journey with their mentees, they find themselves learning, growing, and being inspired in return. From celebrating mentees' achievements to navigating the hurdles they face together, mentors reflect on the rich tapestry of experiences that mentoring provides.

For instance, Michael, a seasoned engineer who has mentored numerous young professionals, shares, "Seeing a mentee overcome a challenge or reach a goal they thought was out of reach is incredibly rewarding. It's not just about imparting technical knowledge but also about fostering resilience and confidence." Michael's reflections underscore the deep satisfaction that comes from witnessing mentees' growth and realizing the pivotal role a mentor can play in that process.

Similarly, Esther, a mentor in a women's leadership program, speaks to the challenges and rewards of mentorship, "Guiding young women as they navigate their careers and personal growth has been both challenging and incredibly fulfilling. Each mentee's journey brings new lessons about patience, understanding, and the power of encouragement."

The Mentor's Growth: while the benefits of mentorship for mentees are well-documented, the impact on mentors themselves is equally significant. Engaging in mentorship offers mentors opportunities for reflection, learning, and personal development. Through the act of mentoring, they refine their communication and leadership skills, gain fresh perspectives, and rekindle their passion for their own careers and lives.

John, a mentor to aspiring entrepreneurs, shares, "Mentoring has pushed me to stay current and innovative. Explaining concepts to my mentees forces me to look at things from new angles, keeping my own entrepreneurial spirit alive." This sentiment is echoed by many mentors who find that the mentorship experience reinvigorates their professional enthusiasm and commitment.

Moreover, the mentorship journey often leads to profound personal insights. As mentors help mentees navigate their paths, they are prompted to reflect on their own journeys, values, and goals. Linda, who mentors young artists, reflects, "Mentoring has taught me as much about myself as it has about guided others. It's a reminder of why I fell in love with art in the first place and has deepened my appreciation for the creative process."

The testimonials from mentors reveal mentorship as a dynamic exchange—a process that enriches and transforms both mentor and mentee. Through sharing their experiences, mentors highlight the multifaceted nature of mentorship, characterized by reciprocal growth, shared challenges, and collective achievements. As these reflections show, mentorship is not just a contribution to others' development but a valuable journey of self-discovery and professional rejuvenation for the mentors themselves. In the landscape of mentorship, everyone grows, learns, and finds new inspiration, making it a truly enriching experience for all involved.

Testimonials From Mentees

At the heart of every mentorship story lies a journey of transformation, where guidance blossoms into achievement, and potential is realized through the dedicated support of a mentor. Testimonials from mentees not only illuminate the tangible outcomes of these mentorship relationships but also offer a deeply personal glimpse into the profound impact mentors have on the lives of those they guide. This section is dedicated to the voices of mentees, sharing their experiences of growth, gratitude, and the milestones reached through the power of mentorship.

From Guidance to Achievement: for many mentees, the mentorship journey is a pivotal experience that opens doors to new opportunities, fostering academic success, career advancements, and significant personal development. These accounts highlight the transformative power of mentorship in action.

Sophia, a recent university graduate, reflects on her experience, "My mentor not only helped me navigate my academic challenges but also guided me towards incredible internship opportunities. Thanks to her support, I've landed my dream job in environmental science." Sophia's story is a testament to the direct impact mentorship can have on a mentee's career path, turning aspirations into tangible successes.

Similarly, Mark shares, "Mentorship was the catalyst for my personal growth. My mentor's encouragement and advice helped me overcome my self-doubt, leading me to start my own business —a goal I once thought was unattainable." Stories like Mark's underscore the role of mentorship in fostering self-confidence and entrepreneurial spirit among mentees.

Gratitude and Recognition: beyond the achievements and milestones, mentees often express profound gratitude towards their mentors and the mentorship programs that brought them together. This gratitude stems not only from the successes achieved but also from the sense of belonging, understanding, and encouragement fostered through the mentorship relationship.

Fatou, who was part of a mentorship program focused on leadership development, shares, "I am immensely grateful for my mentor's wisdom and unwavering support. She believed in me when I struggled to believe in myself, and for that, I am forever thankful." This sentiment of gratitude is echoed by many mentees who recognize the invaluable role their mentors have played in their personal and professional journeys.

Moreover, mentees often acknowledge the broader impact of mentorship programs, appreciating the opportunity to be part of a supportive community that champions growth and development. Ahmed notes, "Being part of this mentorship program has not only accelerated my career but also connected me with a network of peers and professionals who continue to inspire and support me."

The testimonials from mentees paint a vivid picture of mentorship as a transformative force, capable of guiding individuals from potential to achievement. Through their stories of academic success, career advancements, and personal milestones, mentees highlight the instrumental role mentors play in their lives. Beyond the accomplishments, the expressions of gratitude and recognition towards mentors and mentorship programs underscore the deep, lasting impact of these relationships. Mentorship, as experienced by these mentees, is more than just guidance—it's a powerful catalyst for change, growth, and fulfillment.

The Ripple Effect Of Mentorship

The transformative power of mentorship extends far beyond the individual relationships between mentors and mentees, creating a ripple effect that reverberates throughout communities and generations. This phenomenon, where the impact of mentorship multiplies and spreads, underscores the sustainability and expansive potential of mentorship programs. It is a testament to how mentorship can cultivate a culture of continual growth, support, and communal upliftment. This section explores the dynamic legacy of mentorship, focusing on the journey of mentees who transition into mentors and the creation of expansive networks of support that foster a pervasive culture of mentorship.

One of the most compelling outcomes of effective mentorship programs is the evolution of mentees into mentors. This natural progression is a hallmark of the mentorship lifecycle, illustrating its capacity for self-perpetuation and long-term impact. Stories of former mentees who step into mentoring roles illuminate the profound influence that mentorship has on individuals, inspiring them to pay forward the guidance and support they received.

For instance, Clara, once a mentee in a leadership development program, now mentors young women aspiring to careers in STEM. Reflecting on her transition, Clara shares, "My mentor opened up a world of possibilities for me, and now I'm determined to do the same for others. It's my way of giving back and ensuring that the cycle of empowerment continues." Clara's story exemplifies the transformative journey from receiving mentorship to providing it, highlighting the generative nature of mentorship experiences.

Beyond individual transformation, mentorship has the remarkable ability to foster broader networks of support and collaboration. These networks, built on the foundational principles of mentorship, extend the benefits of guidance and support across entire communities, creating an ecosystem where knowledge, resources, and opportunities are shared openly.

Mentorship programs often serve as catalysts for these expansive networks, connecting individuals from diverse backgrounds and disciplines. Through formal events, social media groups, and informal gatherings, mentees and mentors alike can engage with a larger community committed to mutual aid and development.

James, a beneficiary of such a network, notes, "Being part of this mentorship program didn't just connect me with my mentor—it introduced me to a community of peers and professionals eager to support each other. It's a network that has become invaluable to my personal and professional growth."

The ripple effect of mentorship manifests in various ways—mentees stepping into mentoring roles, the establishment of robust support networks, and the creation of a culture where mentorship and mutual aid are ingrained values. This culture not only sustains the momentum of mentorship initiatives but also amplifies their impact, ensuring that the benefits of mentorship are accessible to a wider audience.

Moreover, as this culture of mentorship takes root, it encourages a collective approach to addressing community challenges, leveraging the diverse skills, experiences, and energies of its members. This communal approach to mentorship and development exemplifies the potential of mentorship to effect meaningful, lasting change not just in individuals, but in societies at large.

The ripple effect of mentorship underscores its role as a powerful catalyst for individual transformation, community development, and societal progress. Through the inspiring journeys of mentees becoming mentors and the expansion of supportive networks, mentorship programs demonstrate their potential for sustainability and growth. This enduring legacy of mentorship ensures that the seeds of empowerment, once sown, continue to flourish, fostering a culture of continuous learning, support, and communal upliftment.

The reflections and stories shared throughout Chapter 14 illuminate the profound impact mentorship has across Africa. Each narrative reveals lessons of courage, perseverance, and the transformative power inherent in these connections, inviting us to reflect on the extensive influence of mentorship.

The diverse and inspiring voices from the field go beyond mere success stories. They are vivid testimonies to the growth, contribution, and change possible when individuals are nurtured through support, guidance, and opportunity. These accounts celebrate both personal achievements and collective progress made possible through the mentorship journey, highlighting its role as a catalyst for individual empowerment and societal development.

These personal journeys underscore mentorship's broader societal impact—its ability to nurture leaders, foster innovative solutions to challenges, and cultivate communities of support and understanding. They illustrate how mentorship serves as a cornerstone for building a future where every individual can thrive and contribute to the collective well-being of society.

As we close this chapter, the resonant message is clear: mentorship is an invaluable tool for transformation and growth. The voices from the field do not merely recount individual victories; they echo the vast potential within each person and the significant role mentorship plays in unlocking this potential. These narratives stand as beacons of hope and inspiration, urging future generations of mentors and mentees to engage in this empowering journey.

Let the voices from the field serve as a guiding light, motivating us all to champion and advocate for mentorship. By doing so, we commit to shaping a future that values growth, embraces change, and fosters the development of the next generation of leaders in Africa and beyond. This call to action is not just an invitation but a mandate to recognize and harness the power of mentorship for the betterment of individuals, communities, and societies at large.

MENTORSHIP AS A TOOL FOR SOCIAL CHANGE IN AFRICA

In the dynamic and diverse landscapes of Africa, mentorship emerges as a powerful guiding light for social change, weaving through the continent's myriad challenges and boundless opportunities. This chapter embarks on a deep exploration of mentorship's transformative capacity, illustrating how it serves as a pivotal force in empowering individuals, nurturing future leaders, and fostering a culture of innovation and resilience. Through the personal and impactful touch of mentorship, the seeds of change are meticulously sown, promising a future that fully realizes the immense potential of the African continent and its people.

Mentorship programs stand as foundational pillars for a transformative shift across Africa, laying the groundwork to address critical social issues, bridge educational and economic gaps, and empower the youth. By delving into the multifaceted role of mentorship, this chapter highlights its significant impact on driving social innovation, leadership, and sustainable development. It navigates through mentorship's ability to reshape and remold the continent's challenges and opportunities, examining its profound influence on individuals, communities, and the broader societal fabric. Mentorship is celebrated as an indispensable tool in fostering social change, illustrating its capacity to not only transform lives but also to sculpt the social landscape of Africa towards a brighter, more equitable future.

This chapter explores the profound capacity of mentorship to drive social change across the African continent. It delves into the mechanisms through which mentorship can address socio-economic challenges, empower individuals and communities, and contribute to the sustainable development of nations.

Empowering Africa's Youth For Leadership, Innovation, And Societal Change

In my journey with SAYes Youth Mentoring, I've witnessed firsthand the profound impact mentorship can have on empowering Africa's youth for leadership, innovation, and societal change. The transformative power of mentorship lies in its ability to unlock the vast potential within young Africans, enabling them to lead initiatives that drive significant change within their communities and beyond. By focusing on the empowerment of individuals and nurturing future leaders, mentorship programs are actively laying the groundwork for a resilient, innovative, and prosperous African continent.

Central to societal transformation is the empowerment of individuals. Mentorship plays an instrumental role in this dynamic process by offering guidance, advocacy, support, and essential resources. Mentors equip mentees to navigate and surmount obstacles, realize their personal and professional ambitions, and make substantial contributions to their communities. This individual empowerment acts as a catalyst for broader societal change, creating a domino effect where each empowered person becomes a source of inspiration and a driver of progress within their sphere of influence.

Take, for example, Xholani, a young man from a small township in South Africa. Coming from a background marked by limited resources and educational opportunities, Xholani's aspirations seemed out of reach until he was introduced to a mentorship program that matched him with Thabo, a successful local entrepreneur who had overcome similar challenges. Thabo offered Xholani more than just career guidance; he provided a model of what could be achieved. Through regular meetings, Thabo guided Xholani in setting realistic goals, developing a strategic plan for his future, and building the confidence to pursue his dreams. He advocated for him, introducing Xholani to his network and supporting his application for a scholarship that would enable him to attend university.

Armed with Thabo's guidance, advocacy, and support, Xholani not only secured the scholarship but also became an active community leader, initiating projects aimed at improving access to education for other young people in his township. His journey from a mentee to a community catalyst showcases how mentorship can empower individuals to overcome barriers, achieve their goals, and contribute meaningfully to their communities. Xholani's transformation illustrates the domino effect of empowerment through mentorship. As he was inspired and supported to realize his potential, Xholani became a source of inspiration and support for others, extending the impact of mentorship beyond his personal success to foster broader societal change. His story exemplifies how the empowerment of a single individual through mentorship can catalyze a cycle of growth, inspiration, and progress within a community.

Africa's trajectory towards a brighter future is intricately linked to the quality of its leadership. Recognizing this, mentorship programs are dedicated to nurturing the next generation of visionary leaders. Through mentorship, young Africans are imbued with critical insights, leadership skills, and the confidence to lead with integrity and determination. These emerging leaders are prepared not just to dream of a better future but to actively mobilize and steer their communities and nations towards these aspirational visions.

Consider the story of Kofi, a bright but under-resourced student from Ghana who always harbored dreams of making a significant impact in his community but lacked the guidance and resources to bring his visions to life. That changed when he joined a mentorship program focused on cultivating leadership and fostering innovation, where he was paired with Ama, a renowned tech entrepreneur known for her contributions to Ghana's burgeoning tech scene. Ama introduced Kofi to the world of technology and entrepreneurship, sharing her journey and the lessons she learned along the way. She encouraged Kofi to think critically about the challenges facing his community and to see these challenges as opportunities for innovation. Together, they brainstormed potential tech-based solutions to improve local access to clean water.

Inspired by Ama's mentorship, Kofi developed a prototype for a low-cost water purification device using locally sourced materials. Ama helped him refine his idea, connect with potential investors, and navigate the startup ecosystem. Through this process, Kofi not only honed his leadership skills but also became a young innovator driving social change. Kofi's project soon garnered attention, leading to support from local and international organizations. His success story became a beacon of inspiration for other young Africans, showing that with the right mentorship, Africa's youth can lead and innovate in ways that address pressing societal needs.

Kofi's story demonstrates how mentorship programs that emphasize leadership development and innovation can equip Africa's youth with the skills and confidence to become future change-makers. By connecting mentees with experienced professionals who can guide and inspire them, these programs not only foster individual growth but also contribute to the broader goal of technological advancement and social innovation across the continent.

The strategic engagement of Africa's youth in mentorship programs signifies a powerful commitment to the continent's future. By empowering individuals to overcome challenges, nurturing innovative thinkers, and cultivating ethical leaders, mentorship serves as a potent tool for social change. This holistic approach ensures that the seeds of transformation sown today will blossom into the sustainable development and prosperity of Africa tomorrow. Through mentorship, we are not just shaping the leaders of the future; we are empowering the architects of a new and vibrant African narrative.

Bridging Educational And Economic Gaps Through Mentorship In Africa

Mentorship in Africa stands as a transformative force, bridging significant educational and economic gaps that challenge the continent's growth. Through its strategic application, mentorship provides underserved populations with crucial access to education and economic opportunities, empowering individuals, and propelling societies forward.

Mentorship extends beyond traditional education, offering personalized academic support that addresses specific needs and challenges encountered by African students. This support is vital in areas where educational resources are lacking, and the quality of schooling may be compromised. Through the guidance of mentors, students can overcome these barriers, stay engaged, and achieve their academic goals. Moreover, mentorship fosters a lifelong appreciation for learning and critical thinking skills, essential for navigating the complexities of the modern world. Consider the impact of mentorship programs that connect students with mentors in their fields of interest. Such connections can drastically broaden their academic and professional horizons, increase their aspirations, and provide clear pathways to success.

Beyond educational achievements, mentorship is instrumental in economic empowerment. It introduces young people to career guidance, professional development, and networking opportunities, equipping them with the skills necessary to thrive in the workforce or embark on entrepreneurial ventures. This is particularly crucial in combating the high rates of youth unemployment and underemployment across the continent. Mentors with industry experience play a vital role by sharing insights into market trends and job market realities, thus preparing mentees for successful careers. Mentorship programs focused on entrepreneurship are especially valuable, inspiring young Africans to transform innovative ideas into viable businesses. These programs often provide essential training in financial literacy and business planning and may offer access to funding sources, lowering the barriers young entrepreneurs commonly face.

Mentorship in Africa is more than a catalyst for individual success; it is a cornerstone for broader societal transformation. By enhancing access to quality education, it lights a path to academic excellence for countless young people. Simultaneously, it lays the groundwork for robust economic development by fostering a culture of innovation and entrepreneurship. The mentorship bridge not only spans educational and economic divides but also supports the sustainable development and prosperity of entire communities.

Through dedicated mentorship initiatives, Africa is nurturing a generation poised to lead and innovate. These young leaders are equipped to not only face their local challenges but also contribute to global solutions, showcasing the power of mentorship to effect substantial and lasting change. As these programs continue to evolve and expand, their potential to unlock the immense capabilities of Africa's youth becomes increasingly apparent, promising a future where the continent's potential is fully realized.

Promoting Gender Equality And Social Inclusion Through Mentorship

Mentorship programs in Africa are becoming increasingly crucial tools for promoting gender equality and social inclusion. They challenge longstanding societal norms and provide vital opportunities for empowerment, particularly for women and girls, and marginalized communities.

Empowerment of women and girls through mentorship is key to dismantling entrenched gender norms and advancing equality. These programs are tailored to overcome specific barriers that women and girls face in education, employment, and community engagement. More than just offering academic and career guidance, these initiatives foster safe environments for personal growth, self-expression, and leadership development.

Programs like "Women Lead Africa" illustrate this well. They connect young women with established female leaders across various fields, providing mentees with relatable role models who defy traditional gender roles. These relationships are powerful: they challenge stereotypes, build confidence, and inspire women to pursue leadership roles, driving profound community and societal changes.

Inclusivity is also fundamental to the effectiveness of mentorship programs. Recognizing the varied challenges faced by individuals from economically disadvantaged backgrounds, those with disabilities, or those living in remote areas is crucial. Programs designed with inclusivity in mind ensure that all individuals, regardless of their circumstances, have access to necessary support and resources.

For instance, the "Access for All" initiative provides a poignant example by offering mentorship to young people with disabilities. It delivers practical support to help them navigate daily challenges and encourages them to pursue their ambitions. Similarly, programs targeting youth in remote or underserved areas work to bridge the digital divide and provide these young people with access to educational and economic opportunities that would otherwise be out of reach.

The concerted effort to integrate gender equality and social inclusion into mentorship programs is not just transforming individual lives but is also reshaping communities across Africa. By empowering women and ensuring inclusivity, these programs lay the groundwork for a more equitable society. They equip individuals with the tools and confidence to surmount barriers and contribute to a culture of equality, respect, and mutual support.

The ongoing growth and evolution of these initiatives are vital for nurturing a generation that can lead with innovation and inclusivity, driving Africa towards a more prosperous and equitable future. As mentorship programs continue to expand their reach and deepen their impact, their role in crafting a more inclusive African narrative remains both critical and inspiring.

Strengthening Community Cohesion And Resilience Through Mentorship

Mentorship in Africa goes beyond personal development, deeply influencing community cohesion and resilience. It's more than a process; it's a transformative journey that weaves the fabric of communities tighter, fostering strength and unity in the face of adversity.

In the heart of African communities, mentorship is a vibrant tradition, a communal endeavor that emphasizes collective success. It's about creating a support network where knowledge and experiences are shared, thereby strengthening social capital. Social capital isn't just a buzzword—it's the glue that holds societies together through networks of relationships, trust, and mutual understanding.

Community-based mentorship programs brilliantly highlight how young individuals can stay rooted in their traditions while reaching new heights. By connecting young people with seasoned local leaders, these programs impart wisdom and reinforce communal bonds. Mentees learn about personal and professional growth while absorbing the essence of civic responsibility and communal welfare.

The resilience of a community—its capacity to recover from economic, social, or environmental shocks—is deeply intertwined with the robustness of its social structures. Mentorship, especially in regions prone to challenges like environmental degradation or economic instability, prepares communities to thrive, not just survive.

Programs that focus on sustainable practices and disaster preparedness, such as "Resilient Youth Africa," demonstrate mentorship's role in readying communities for environmental challenges. By connecting young people with sustainability experts, these programs educate and empower communities to lead proactive change, enhancing their resilience.

Economic mentorship initiatives also transform communities from within. By nurturing entrepreneurial skills and providing access to economic resources, mentorship sparks a cycle of growth and stability. This type of mentorship doesn't just create job opportunities; it builds an ecosystem where innovation and economic growth can flourish, strengthening the community's economic backbone.

The narrative of mentorship in Africa is a powerful testament to its role as a catalyst for community development and societal progress. Through each mentor-mentee relationship, seeds of change are planted, promising not only individual growth but the flourishing of entire communities. As these mentorship programs evolve, they continue to empower more individuals, enriching the community reservoir of knowledge and skills.

This dynamic process underscores the significance of mentorship in sculpting resilient, cohesive, and prosperous communities across Africa. It's about crafting a legacy of interconnectedness, resilience, and mutual upliftment—a testament to the power of collective effort and shared vision in driving societal change.

In every village and city, from the plains to the bustling metropolises, the impact of mentorship reverberates, echoing the strength of unity and the potential of each individual nurtured within a supportive community. This is the heart of mentorship in Africa: a journey of shared growth, mutual respect, and unwavering support, building a brighter, more resilient future for all.

Mentorship Programs As A Strategy To Combat Youth Crime In Africa

Across Africa, where the specter of youth involvement in crime looms large, mentorship programs are proving to be a transformative force, reshaping lives, and redirecting young individuals towards more positive futures. The narrative isn't just about crime prevention; it's a broader story of hope, opportunity, and community rebuilding.

Imagine growing up in a neighborhood where opportunities are scarce and paths to success even scarcer. Here, mentorship introduces young people to role models who've walked similar paths but have found success and fulfillment. These mentors don't just guide, support, and advocacy; they inspire, showing that alternatives to crime exist and are achievable. They embody the adage that seeing is believing, providing a tangible example that life can be different.

Mentorship fills the void that idleness breeds by engaging youth in activities that enrich their skills and boost their self-worth. Whether it's learning a trade, excelling academically, or participating in community service, these programs provide structured environments where young people can thrive. By channeling their energy into constructive activities, the allure of criminal endeavors diminishes.

Beyond practical skills, mentorship nurtures emotional and social growth. Communication, empathy, and problem-solving are cultivated skills that equip the youth to face life's challenges without resorting to crime. These programs offer safe spaces for expression and support, helping to alleviate the frustrations and alienations that can drive criminal behavior.

Effective mentorship programs do more than connect individuals; they weave stronger community networks. These connections foster a sense of belonging and responsibility—vital in nurturing a community ethos that rejects crime. When young people feel invested in their communities, they're less likely to harm them.

Focusing on education and career guidance, mentorship programs directly enhance young people's prospects. Better education leads to better job opportunities, which can steer youth away from the economic motivations of crime. By improving individual prospects, these programs help lift entire communities.

Consider the story of John from South Africa—a former gang member turned mentor. Through his participation in a local mentorship program, John changed course, pursued an education in law enforcement, and now helps guide other at-risk youths. His story is a testament to the program's impact, not just on individuals but on the broader community, reducing crime and fostering a new generation of community leaders.

Mentorship programs in Africa are not just initiatives; they are lifelines that pull many away from the brink, guiding them to safer, more productive paths. They are about building the kind of society where every young person can see a future for themselves within the law. Through ongoing support, skills training, and positive role modeling, these programs don't just change individual lives—they can transform entire communities, making them more resilient, prosperous, and secure. In embracing mentorship, there's a clear message: Africa's youth are not the problem; they are the solution. With the right guidance, they can and will be the architects of a brighter African future.

Overcoming Educational And Employment Barriers Through Mentorship

Mentorship in Africa represents a lifeline, bridging daunting educational and employment barriers that many young people face. Picture a vast landscape where potential and opportunity stretch as far as the eye can see, yet countless hurdles stand in the way. This is where mentorship steps in, not just as a guide but as a transformative force that equips the continent's youth with the tools they need for success.

In Africa, systemic obstacles often impede access to quality education and viable employment. Many young Africans find themselves constrained by limited educational resources or lack of exposure to career pathways. Mentorship programs like Scholars Africa exemplify proactive efforts to counter these issues. By linking students with academic mentors globally, these programs extend educational opportunities beyond local limitations, preparing students for competitive roles in the global marketplace. Moreover, career mentorship provides invaluable insights into diverse industries, offering guidance that aligns educational achievements with market demands and opportunities.

The effectiveness of mentorship also hinges on its cultural sensitivity and acceptance within local communities. Challenges arise when traditional norms conflict with the new paradigms introduced by mentorship initiatives. Success in this aspect involves incorporating respected local leaders as mentors and integrating culturally relevant practices within the mentorship frameworks. Such strategies ensure that the programs are not only respectful of cultural values but are also embraced by the communities they intend to serve. This local endorsement strengthens the mentor-mentee relationships, making the mentorship's impacts more profound and sustainable.

The potential for scaling up mentorship programs in Africa is immense. Strategic expansion involves leveraging technology to enhance accessibility and forming partnerships with educational institutions and industries to broaden the scope of mentorship. Such expansion not only increases the reach of these programs but also their impact, enabling them to support more young individuals across varied regions. Additionally, engaging the African diaspora as mentors could further enrich these programs with diverse experiences and global perspectives, adding depth to the mentorship available.

Think of the journey of a young individual in Africa who, through mentorship, gains not only academic and career guidance but also a renewed sense of confidence and purpose. This is the story of countless youths whose horizons have been broadened through these programs. Mentorship does more than fill gaps—it builds bridges to futures filled with hope and promise.

As mentorship continues to evolve, its significance in shaping not just individuals but entire communities and the broader economic landscape of Africa cannot be overstated. With each mentorship session, workshop, and community engagement, the foundations for a resilient, empowered, and progressive society are strengthened. In embracing mentorship, Africa is not just preparing its youth for the challenges of today but is equipping them to be the leaders and innovators of tomorrow. This ongoing commitment to mentorship is essential for realizing the vast potential of Africa's youth, ensuring they not only ascend to meet their personal aspirations but also drive the continent toward greater heights of development and prosperity.

Optimal Venues For Mentorship Programs In Africa

In exploring the landscape of mentorship across Africa, the choice of venue plays a crucial role in determining the effectiveness and impact of these programs. Whether it's in schools, workplaces, community centers, or through innovative online platforms, each setting provides unique opportunities to foster growth and development among Africa's youth.

Starting with schools, they are foundational in nurturing young minds. Integrating mentorship programs within educational institutions allows for early intervention, helping to identify and nurture the talents and challenges of students from a young age. This proactive approach in schools can significantly enhance academic engagement, boost retention rates, and instill a lifelong passion for learning. The structured environment of schools also makes it an ideal setting for providing consistent and impactful mentorship, addressing both academic and personal development needs.

Moving into the professional world, workplaces serve as a critical platform for mentorship, especially for young professionals and budding entrepreneurs. In these settings, mentorship bridges the gap between theoretical knowledge acquired in educational settings and the practical skills needed in the real world. For young employees and entrepreneurs, having a mentor in the workplace or through professional networks can accelerate career development, improve job satisfaction, and foster a culture of continuous learning and innovation within organizations.

Community centers, on the other hand, offer a more informal but equally impactful venue for mentorship. These centers reach a wider audience, including those not currently engaged in formal education or employment such as out-of-school youth, women, and other marginalized groups. Programs run in community centers can focus on personal development, civic engagement, and life skills, promoting social inclusion and community solidarity.

In today's digital age, online platforms have become indispensable in overcoming geographical barriers, connecting mentors and mentees across different regions and even continents. Virtual mentorship programs leverage technology to offer flexible and inclusive access to mentorship opportunities, ranging from academic support to personal development workshops. This digital approach ensures that anyone with internet access can benefit from mentorship, regardless of their physical location.

By considering the unique advantages of each venue, mentorship programs can be tailored to meet the diverse needs of Africa's youth. Whether through the structured environment of schools, the professional setting of workplaces, the inclusive spaces of community centers, or the expansive reach of online platforms, mentorship is a versatile tool. It's about creating a multifaceted ecosystem of support that not only addresses the specific challenges faced by individuals but also harnesses the collective potential of communities across Africa. This integrated approach to mentorship is key to empowering the next generation of African leaders, innovators, and change-makers, driving societal transformation and sustainable development across the continent.

Reflecting on the transformative journey of mentorship across Africa fills me with a profound sense of hope and possibility. Mentorship here has transcended its traditional roles, morphing into a potent instrument for societal transformation—a tool that not only shapes futures but also redefines communities and strengthens the very fabric of society.

Throughout this exploration, the narratives have woven a vivid tapestry showcasing mentorship as a dynamic catalyst for empowerment and leadership development. These stories highlight its crucial role in bridging significant educational and economic gaps, fostering innovation, and steering Africa toward a future rich with equality, prosperity, and sustainability.

Mentorship is fundamentally about connection—about the rich exchange that happens when experienced individuals invest in the growth of another, proving that everyone has something invaluable to learn and something impactful to teach. At this pivotal moment, as Africa stands on the cusp of a new era of growth and development, the strategic enhancement and expansion of mentorship programs across the continent are not just beneficial; they are imperative. It is through these programs that individuals will not only realize their own potential but also become pivotal agents of change within their communities, thereby contributing to broader social advancement and resilience.

Looking forward, the path is clear: there is a pressing need for a collaborative approach that unites governments, the private sector, educational institutions, and communities. Together, they must forge a shared mission to nurture environments where mentorship can thrive, deeply embedded within the societal fabric. By doing so, Africa can harness the collective strengths and aspirations of its people, paving the way for a future that not only celebrates diversity and fosters innovation but also champions social justice.

As we conclude this exploration, we are reminded of the far-reaching impacts of mentorship—not just in changing individual lives but in sparking a movement of enduring social change across Africa. The commitment to nurturing and expanding mentorship programs stands as a commitment to building a continent defined by empowered individuals, cohesive communities, and an unwavering drive towards progress and equity. Within mentorship lies the seeds of Africa's renaissance—a promise of growth, unity, and a brighter tomorrow for all.

SCALING UP AND SUSTAINABILITY OF MENTORSHIP PROGRAMS

The journey of mentorship in Africa has showcased its incredible power, underscoring its effectiveness in nurturing talent, fostering leadership, and catalyzing social change. As more success stories emerge and their impacts deepen, it's becoming crucial to expand these programs, ensuring their reach and transformative influence extend across broader communities and nations. However, scaling up introduces a myriad of challenges, such as maintaining the quality of the programs, securing financial sustainability, and keeping the personal engagement that is pivotal to effective mentorship.

In this chapter, we explore essential strategies for effectively scaling up and sustaining mentorship initiatives. It's about striking a careful balance between broadening the reach and maintaining the essence of these programs. We'll examine various successful models from across the continent, discussing innovative approaches to secure funding, forge partnerships, integrate technology, and adapt programs to ensure they not only grow in scope but also remain vibrant, impactful, and sustainable over the long haul.

As we delve into this discussion, our objective is clear: to provide a comprehensive roadmap for mentorship programs aiming to expand while staying true to their foundational mission of empowering individuals and transforming societies. The ultimate vision is a robust and adaptable mentorship ecosystem that thrives over time, ensuring the seeds of change planted today continue to blossom and enrich the lives of future generations across Africa.

Strategies For Expanding Mentorship Initiatives

Expanding mentorship initiatives across Africa has been one of the most rewarding endeavors I've undertaken. The drive to magnify their impact means reaching more lives and fostering greater societal change, a journey that is as challenging as it is fulfilling. This growth, however, demands a blend of strategic planning, keen adaptation, and genuine collaboration.

Any successful expansion starts with a thorough assessment. Evaluating what works and what doesn't, understanding the unique demands of new settings—whether it's shifting from urban to rural environments, or vice versa—is crucial. The ability to adapt while keeping the essence of the program intact allows us to reach different communities without losing the core of what makes our programs effective.

I've learned that no initiative thrives in isolation. Partnering with local governments, non-profits, educational bodies, and the private sector has opened new avenues for resources and expansion. These alliances not only bring financial support but also local insights and an extended reach into communities. Such collaborations can, for example, integrate mentorship into educational systems, directly impacting students within their own learning environments.

The digital revolution has been a game-changer. Utilizing online platforms has allowed us to transcend geographical limitations, connecting mentors and mentees across vast distances. Digital tools not only facilitate communication and training but also create communities of support for mentees and mentors alike. Furthermore, the use of social media and mobile apps enhances visibility and access, drawing more participants into our programs.

The heart of sustainability in mentorship lies in local empowerment. By training local leaders and mentors, we ensure that the programs are delivered in ways that resonate culturally and contextually with each new community. These local figures become pillars of the mentorship program, embodying the mission and driving its success on the ground.

This approach to scaling mentorship initiatives is not just about reaching more people but deepening the impact of each connection made. It's about setting the stage for a future where mentorship is not an exception but a norm, embedded in the fabric of societies across Africa. Through thoughtful expansion, strategic partnerships, and a commitment to local leadership, we are paving the way for a generation that is empowered, connected, and ready to lead. This journey, though fraught with challenges, is one of the most profound ways we can contribute to shaping a continent marked by diversity, innovation, and resilience.

Ensuring The Longevity And Impact Of Programs

Ensuring the longevity and impact of mentorship programs is much like nurturing a tree in a garden—both require ongoing care, strategic nurturing, and adaptation to the changing seasons to thrive. This story-like reflection encapsulates my experiences and observations in managing and guiding mentorship initiatives that aim to foster sustainable personal growth and societal transformation across Africa.

The key to longevity begins with creating a sustainable funding model. It's much like ensuring our tree has enough water and nutrients to grow year after year. Traditional funding through grants and donations provides the roots for stability, but integrating social entrepreneurship brings a rejuvenating innovation. By creating products or services that align with the mission, programs not only sustain themselves financially but also embed deeper into the community's economic and social fabric. This dual approach helps the program remain relevant and impactful, ensuring it can continue to support the community effectively.

Just as a gardener regularly checks the health of their plants, continuous monitoring and evaluation are vital for mentorship programs. This ongoing process, involving both the collection of quantifiable data and qualitative feedback from participants, allows us to understand what's flourishing and what might need more attention or a changed approach. Such evaluations keep the program aligned with its goals and responsive to the needs of those it serves, while also demonstrating its value—crucial for securing ongoing support from stakeholders.

Community engagement and ownership are akin to the soil that surrounds our tree—rich, supportive, and essential for growth. When the local community is involved in every stage of the program, from planning through to evaluation, the initiatives reflect the community's own values and needs. This involvement fosters a strong sense of ownership and commitment, crucial for the program's sustainability. Engaged communities provide a supportive environment, much like fertile soil supports a tree, enabling the program to flourish.

Finally, adaptability and resilience are the program's ability to withstand storms and droughts. Just as environmental conditions affect a tree, social, economic, and political changes can impact mentorship programs. Programs must therefore be designed with flexibility to adapt to these changes, ensuring they remain relevant and effective. This might mean adjusting focus areas, adopting new technologies, or finding innovative ways to engage participants and stakeholders.

Navigating these elements effectively ensures that mentorship programs not only endure but also expand their reach and impact, much like a tree that grows to provide shade and fruit for many around it. As we look to the future, these mentorship programs stand as beacons of hope and catalysts for change, nurturing a new generation of leaders and innovators who are equipped to tackle the challenges and seize the opportunities that lie ahead for Africa. This commitment to nurturing and expanding mentorship initiatives is a commitment to cultivating a thriving, resilient community, ready to grow and prosper in an ever-changing landscape.

The unfolding story of mentorship programs across Africa is not just a narrative about personal growth and professional development; it's a broader saga of societal transformation. These initiatives, which I have seen nurturing the continent's youth, are preparing them to lead their communities towards a brighter, more resilient future. As we wrap up this exploration into the scaling and sustainability of these programs, it becomes clear that the road ahead, while filled with challenges, is also ripe with potential.

Scaling up these programs isn't just a matter of increasing numbers. It involves strategic thinking and careful planning to ensure that as they grow, they retain their effectiveness and continue to resonate deeply with their participants. The commitment to expanding mentorship must be matched with robust and innovative funding strategies that secure financial stability without compromising the programs' mission and values. Whether through international grants, local partnerships, or entrepreneurial ventures within the programs themselves, securing diverse funding sources is critical for sustainable growth.

Monitoring and evaluation stand out as essential tools in this journey. They are not merely formalities but are integral to understanding the impact of these programs and guiding their evolution. This continuous feedback loop helps identify what works and what might be improved, ensuring that the mentorship remains relevant and effective even as it reaches more people.

Community engagement is perhaps the cornerstone of sustainability. True resilience is built from the ground up, and for mentorship programs to thrive, they must be rooted in the communities they aim to uplift. This means not just serving these communities but actively involving them in shaping the programs. When community members feel ownership of the mentorship initiatives, they are more invested in their success and sustainability.

Lastly, the ability to adapt and be resilient in the face of changing circumstances—whether economic shifts, political upheaval, or social changes—is what will allow these programs to endure and remain impactful. It's about being flexible enough to navigate obstacles and seize opportunities as they arise.

As this chapter closes, it's clear that the path forward for mentorship programs in Africa is a collaborative one. It requires the dedication of governments, the private sector, NGOs, and the communities themselves. Together, they can ensure that the seeds of mentorship sown today will grow into strong trees under whose shade future generations can thrive. This isn't just an investment in individuals but in the very fabric of society, promising a future where Africa's potential is fully realized, nurtured by the hands of its own people.

THE FUTURE OF MENTORSHIP IN AFRICA

As we look to the horizon of mentorship in Africa, we stand on the cusp of a new era. This chapter peels back the layers of emerging trends and opportunities that are shaping mentorship within this vibrant continent. In the vast and varied landscapes of Africa, mentorship is poised to play a pivotal role in molding the future, intertwining age-old wisdom with the boundless possibilities brought forth by technological advancement and innovation.

Mentorship in Africa is more than just a transfer of knowledge; it is a bridge connecting the rich heritage of the past with the dynamic potential of the future. As digital tools and platforms reshape the educational and professional landscapes, they also redefine the scope and efficacy of mentorship. This chapter explores how the integration of technology into mentorship practices can dramatically enhance their reach and impact, offering new ways to engage, educate, and empower the youth.

Amidst a backdrop of rapid technological change and a burgeoning youth demographic, the need for robust, scalable mentorship programs has never been more pressing. These programs are not just about guiding young minds but about catalyzing societal transformation. This narrative delves into how mentorship can be a formidable tool in addressing the myriad challenges facing Africa today—from skills development to employment and beyond.

Imagine a future where mentorship is seamlessly woven into the fabric of daily life, where every young person in Africa has access to a mentor who not only guides them but also inspires them to achieve their fullest potential. This vision for the future considers how mentorship could evolve to not only adapt to the changing world but to actively shape it, fostering a generation of leaders, innovators, and change-makers who are equipped to navigate and influence the complexities of a global society.

The journey through this chapter is an invitation to dream big and think differently about the role of mentorship in Africa's future—a future that is rich with opportunity, driven by innovation, and anchored in the timeless values of community and support.

Emerging Trends And Opportunities In The Future Of Mentorship In Africa

As we venture into the future of mentorship in Africa, it's exhilarating to see how new trends and opportunities are beginning to shape its landscape. This transformative period is highlighted by an increased focus on empowering the youth, who are the keystones of Africa's socio-economic revolution. With a burgeoning youth demographic ripe with potential, mentorship programs are uniquely positioned to unlock this potential, offering support, guidance, and invaluable opportunities. These initiatives are not just support networks but pivotal platforms for fostering informed, empowered young leaders ready to face the challenges of their times.

Another compelling trend is the rise of cross-sector mentorship programs that integrate knowledge from diverse domains like technology, entrepreneurship, health, and the arts. These interdisciplinary initiatives reflect the complex, interconnected challenges facing the continent, providing mentees with a holistic approach to personal and professional development. Such programs are pioneering innovation and creative problem-solving, preparing young Africans for a dynamic, rapidly evolving global landscape.

Furthermore, there's a significant shift towards enhancing the role of women and girls in mentorship programs. This focus is crucial in addressing the historical barriers that have limited women's opportunities and participation in many sectors. By prioritizing the mentorship of women and girls, these programs not only strive to balance gender inequalities but also enrich the mentorship ecosystem with diverse insights and perspectives. This approach fosters a more inclusive, equitable development path, ensuring that women and girls can achieve their full potential.

The ongoing evolution of mentorship in Africa is marked by a broader shift towards inclusivity and interdisciplinarity, aligning with the continent's multifaceted needs and vast opportunities. The expansion of mentorship is setting the stage for a future where every African youth can access the tools and guidance needed to thrive. This narrative isn't just about growth; it's about paving a sustainable path for empowerment and leadership that transcends generations.

Witnessing these trends unfold, it's clear that mentorship is becoming a cornerstone for nurturing a resilient, innovative future for Africa. The promise of mentorship lies in its ability to transform lives and communities, ensuring that the continent's growth is both shared and sustainable. As these programs continue to adapt and expand, their impact will undoubtedly echo through the ages, heralding a new era of progress and prosperity for Africa.

Integrating Technology And Innovation In Mentorship

As I reflect on the burgeoning role of technology and innovation in mentorship across Africa, it's clear that we are on the cusp of a remarkable transformation. This digital revolution is not just changing how mentorship is conducted; it's expanding its reach and deepening its impact, offering new possibilities for personal growth and societal advancement.

Digital platforms are at the heart of this transformation. They enable mentorship to transcend the traditional barriers of distance and access, connecting mentors and mentees across continents. Imagine a young woman in a remote Kenyan village, engaging in real-time with a seasoned professional in Lagos, getting insights that reshape her career trajectory. This is the power of digital mentorship – making connections that were once impossible, now possible, and fostering a global community of learning and growth.

Social media, too, plays a pivotal role. It's more than just a space for socializing; it's a vibrant community where mentoring relationships can flourish. Platforms like LinkedIn, Twitter, and even Facebook have become hubs where young Africans can find mentorship opportunities, join conversations, and share experiences that span across different cultures and industries. These networks are not only platforms for connection but also springboards for visibility and professional growth.

The adoption of innovative educational tools is another exciting development. Mobile apps designed specifically for mentorship help structure interactions between mentors and mentees, making these exchanges more fruitful. They allow for setting goals, tracking progress, and providing feedback in a structured way. And with the advent of immersive technologies like virtual reality (VR) and augmented reality (AR), mentorship can involve experiences that are engaging and profoundly impactful. Imagine learning about marine biology through a VR dive into the ocean or understanding mechanical engineering by assembling a machine in AR. These technologies make learning vivid and memorable.

Data analytics is transforming mentorship from an art to a science. By harnessing the power of big data, mentorship programs can make informed decisions about matching mentors with mentees, tailoring learning experiences to individual needs, and measuring the effectiveness of mentorship interventions. This approach ensures that each mentoring relationship is as impactful as possible and that the programs themselves continuously evolve based on empirical evidence.

As these technologies integrate more seamlessly into mentorship programs, they not only enhance the learning experience but also ensure that these initiatives are inclusive, effective, and aligned with the future. The journey of integrating technology into mentorship in Africa is just beginning, but its potential is boundless. It promises a future where mentorship is a key driver of development, equipped to prepare Africa's youth for the challenges of a globalized world.

In this era of rapid technological advancement, as we innovate and adapt, the essence of mentorship remains the same: a deeply human endeavor to pass on knowledge, inspire change, and empower the next generation. As Africa harnesses these new tools, the future of mentorship looks not only bright but revolutionary, promising a continent fully empowered to realize its vast potential.

A Vision For The Next Generation

As Africa strides toward a vibrant future, the thread of mentorship weaves through its developmental narrative, becoming a pivotal force in shaping the continent's destiny. This vision for the next generation is anchored deeply in empowering Africa's youth, fostering sustainable development, and nurturing a pervasive culture of mentorship, all designed to unlock a prosperous future.

Empowering Future Leaders: The story begins with Africa's young, brimming with potential and enthusiasm, poised to take the helm. Mentorship stands as a transformative force, arming these young minds with the critical skills, ethical grounding, and creative thinking necessary to navigate complex challenges both locally and globally. Imagine vibrant, driven individuals stepping up as community leaders and innovators, inspired by mentors who have charted similar paths. This isn't just about individual success; it's about cultivating leaders who are committed to societal betterment, equipped to spearhead initiatives that bring about significant social change.

Driving Sustainable Development: Mentorship is a powerful catalyst for sustainable development. Envision mentorship programs meticulously designed to embed sustainability into the core of young minds, preparing them to champion ecological stewardship, economic inclusivity, and social innovation. These programs focus on practical applications of sustainable technologies and strategies, ensuring that the upcoming leaders are not only advocates but active participants in sustainable practices. This approach aligns with the broader goals of the Sustainable Development Goals (SDGs), propelling communities towards enhanced well-being and environmental care.

Cultivating a Mentorship Culture: The future shines brightly on a continent where mentorship is a cultural cornerstone, transcending the conventional frameworks of education and professional development. In this envisioned future, mentorship permeates every layer of society, creating a robust network of support and knowledge sharing. From the bustling markets of Nairobi to the scholarly halls of Cairo, mentorship is recognized as a vital tool for personal growth and communal advancement. Every individual, regardless of age or social standing, both teaches and learns, enriching the collective wisdom of the community.

A Unified Vision for Growth: This narrative of mentorship is not a solitary endeavor but a collective movement towards a unified vision of growth and prosperity. It calls for the collaboration of governments, businesses, educational institutions, and civil societies to invest in mentorship as a priority. By fostering an environment that supports mentorship, these stakeholders ensure that mentorship programs are accessible, impactful, and tailored to meet the evolving needs of the African populace.

This vision, grounded in the principles of mentorship, promises a future where Africa's youth are empowered, communities are resilient, and sustainable development is the norm. Through the concerted efforts of all sectors of society, we can create a future where the transformative power of mentorship is fully realized, guiding Africa towards an era of unprecedented growth and prosperity.

As we look to the future, the role of mentorship in Africa is clear —it is both a beacon of hope and a practical strategy for societal advancement. This envisioned future, where mentorship catalyzes profound growth and innovation, is within reach. It requires commitment, collaboration, and a steadfast belief in the power of mentorship to transform lives. Africa, with its rich history and dynamic present, stands ready to embrace this future, ensuring that its greatest asset—its people—are prepared to lead the continent toward a new era of opportunity and prosperity.

As we stand at the precipice of a new era for Africa, the horizon is bright with the promise of transformation, innovation, and growth. The future of mentorship in Africa, as explored in this chapter, presents a beacon of hope and a strategic blueprint for nurturing the continent's greatest asset—its people. Mentorship, with its profound ability to empower leaders, catalyze social change, and foster sustainable development, is poised to play a pivotal role in Africa's journey towards a brighter future.

This chapter serves as a clarion call to action for stakeholders across the spectrum— governments, private sector entities, educational institutions, non-profits, and individuals alike—to rally behind the cause of mentorship. The collective commitment to nurturing, scaling, and sustaining mentorship programs is essential for unlocking the vast potential that lies within Africa's youth and communities. By embracing emerging trends, harnessing the power of technology and innovation, and prioritizing the empowerment of the next generation, we can ensure that mentorship remains a dynamic force for good.

The vision outlined for mentorship in Africa is not merely aspirational but achievable. It requires a concerted effort, strategic investments, and a shared belief in the transformative power of mentorship. As stakeholders collaborate to expand the reach and deepen the impact of mentorship initiatives, we can look forward to a future where every African has the opportunity to learn, grow, and contribute to the continent's prosperity.

In conclusion, the future of mentorship in Africa is a journey of collective effort and shared destiny. It offers a pathway to a future where mentorship is not just an intervention but a fundamental pillar of societal development—a future where Africa's potential is fully realized through the empowerment of its people. Let us embrace this future with open arms and commit to making mentorship a lasting legacy for generations to come.

POLICY RECOMMENDATIONS

As I explore the interplay between mentorship and entrepreneurship in Africa, the stories of local entrepreneurs who have soared under the guidance of adept mentors resonate deeply with me. These stories not only shed light on the pathway to success but also highlight the critical need for robust policy frameworks that support and nurture these transformative relationships.

Consider Gracy, a fictional character representing many young African entrepreneurs. She has an innovative idea for an agri-tech business that could revolutionize crop yields for small-scale farmers. Yet, despite her potential, Gracy faces daunting barriers: securing funding, accessing markets, and finding robust business guidance. This is where effective policy support becomes essential, transforming potential hurdles into steppingstones for success.

Imagine if our policies could foster an ecosystem rich with opportunities for mentorship. What if we had funding models specifically designed to support mentorship initiatives? Government grants could encourage established entrepreneurs to guide new business owners. Tax incentives could be provided to companies that integrate mentorship into their business models, easing financial burdens and encouraging them to invest in the next generation of entrepreneurs.

Moreover, policies could mandate corporate participation in mentorship, especially in critical sectors such as technology, agriculture, and manufacturing. Such policies would not only enhance corporate social responsibility but also ensure that the invaluable knowledge of experienced professionals is passed down.

Creating an enabling environment goes beyond financial and regulatory incentives; it's about nurturing a culture that values mentorship. This could be fostered through public recognition of successful mentor-mentee relationships and integrating mentorship training into the educational curriculum. This approach prepares young professionals to seek and provide mentorship throughout their careers.

Additionally, in our interconnected world, policies supporting cross-border mentorship could connect African entrepreneurs with a global pool of mentors, expanding their horizons and resources.

The vision laid out in this chapter is ambitious but achievable with committed action from policymakers. By fostering an environment supportive of mentorship-driven entrepreneurship, we are paving the way for a future where African entrepreneurs are leaders on the global stage. This commitment to nurturing and expanding mentorship programs is a commitment to building a more prosperous and equitable Africa, where individuals like Amina can turn their innovative ideas into reality, contributing significantly to both local and global economies.

Funding Models And Financial Support

Reflecting on the burgeoning entrepreneurial spirit across Africa, I often think about how vital mentorship is in nurturing this energy into something transformative. One of the pivotal ways to encourage this nurturing is through well-thought-out funding models and financial support systems that not only sustain but also expand mentorship programs.

Imagine a world where governments actively recognize and support the power of mentorship by establishing dedicated funds specifically for this purpose. These funds could be directed towards programs that connect seasoned entrepreneurs with novices, facilitating a transfer of knowledge and skills that is invaluable. Such government grants would not only bolster the mentorship programs but also signal a commitment to fostering an ecosystem of continuous learning and entrepreneurial spirit.

Additionally, envision a policy where businesses receive tangible benefits for participating in mentorship. Tax incentives for companies that engage in such programs could be a game-changer. These incentives could take various forms, such as tax deductions or credits, aligned with the level of involvement in mentorship activities. This would not only ease the financial burden on businesses but also motivate them to invest more in developing the next generation of leaders and innovators.

Through these stories, it's clear that financial strategies like dedicated funding and tax incentives are more than just economic tools; they are vital cogs in the machinery that drives mentorship and, by extension, broad societal growth. By investing in mentorship, we're not just fostering individual success stories; we're cultivating an environment ripe for innovation and equipped to tackle the challenges of tomorrow. This vision of structured financial support could very well be the backbone that mentorship programs across Africa need to thrive and impact more lives, shaping the continent's future one entrepreneur at a time.

Development Of Policies That Encourage Corporate Mentorship Programs

As we look across the vibrant economic landscape of Africa, there's a compelling story to be told about the power of mentorship within the corporate sector. Imagine, if you will, a scenario where governments step into craft policies that don't just encourage but require companies in critical sectors like technology, agriculture, and manufacturing to engage in mentorship activities. This could become an integral part of their Corporate Social Responsibility (CSR) initiatives.

Take the tech industry, for example, a sector burgeoning with innovation and growth potential. Here, seasoned professionals possess a wealth of knowledge that could significantly benefit the next generation of digital pioneers. By mandating tech companies to implement mentorship programs, we can ensure that this invaluable knowledge is passed down, not just maintaining the industry's growth but accelerating it.

Similarly, in agriculture, where much of Africa's economy takes root, experienced agronomists and business leaders could provide mentorship to young entrepreneurs aiming to innovate farming techniques and sustainability practices. This transfer of knowledge could lead to improved food security and economic stability across the continent.

Manufacturing also stands to gain from such policies. With much of the world looking to diversify production lines outside traditional markets, Africa's manufacturing sector is poised for expansion.

By integrating mentorship into this sector, we can equip a new generation of manufacturers with the skills and insights needed to compete on a global scale, driving economic growth and creating jobs.

These policies wouldn't just be regulatory mandates; they would represent a strategic investment in the continent's future. By requiring companies to dedicate time and resources to mentorship, governments can cultivate a culture of continuous professional development and innovation.

Imagine a future where every major company contributes to a national mentorship initiative, creating an interconnected network of professional guidance and support. This would not only enhance the employability and skills of young Africans but also solidify the corporate sector's role in societal development.

Such a policy initiative requires careful planning and collaboration between the public and private sectors. It would involve setting clear guidelines on what constitutes effective mentorship and how these programs should be implemented to align with broader economic and social goals. Additionally, it would necessitate ongoing monitoring and evaluation to ensure these mentorship activities yield the desired outcomes.

By fostering a policy environment that values and promotes corporate mentorship, we can significantly amplify the impact of Africa's economic sectors, preparing a robust pipeline of skilled professionals ready to lead the continent towards a more prosperous and sustainable future.

Enhancing Mentorship Culture

In our collective journey toward nurturing a culture of growth and development, the importance of mentorship cannot be overstated. It's not just about the exchange of knowledge; it's about creating a supportive ecosystem that fosters long-term personal and professional growth. Let's envision a community where mentorship is deeply valued—a community that not only encourages the seeking of guidance but also celebrates the giving of it. This vision involves more than just the occasional workshop; it involves a systematic approach to embedding mentorship into the very fabric of our society.

Consider the power of public recognition. It's not merely about awards or ceremonial mentions. Imagine a scenario where stories of impactful mentor-mentee relationships are regularly highlighted through media campaigns, showcased in newsletters, or featured at major community events. These stories wouldn't just serve to congratulate; they would inspire others by illustrating the tangible benefits and transformative potential of mentorship. Such initiatives could elevate the status of mentorship to that of other respected community contributions, like volunteerism or civic leadership.

Now, picture our educational systems embracing mentorship as a core component of their curricula. From primary schools to tertiary institutions, integrating mentorship training can prepare young individuals not only to be receptive to guidance but also to provide it. Workshops on effective communication, understanding individual differences, and leadership could be woven into existing programs, creating a pipeline of skilled mentors who are just as prepared to teach as they are to learn.

This integrated approach does more than prepare individuals for the workforce; it prepares them to contribute positively to their communities. It ensures that as professionals progress in their careers, they are equipped not only with technical skills but with a mentor's acumen—ready to guide the next generation and give back to the community that fostered their growth.

Beyond formal programs, fostering a mentorship culture means creating spaces that encourage informal mentorship relationships. This could involve setting up mentorship corners in community centers, libraries, and even online platforms where experienced individuals can offer impromptu guidance and support to those looking to learn.

By championing these initiatives, we can transform the landscape of mentorship in Africa. It's about creating an environment where mentorship is as fundamental as any other educational or professional pursuit—a vital element of societal infrastructure that supports a cycle of continual learning and mutual growth.

This vision is ambitious, but it's far from unattainable. With committed action from policymakers, educators, and community leaders, we can cultivate an environment that not only supports but thrives on the principles of mentorship. This is how we build a future where every individual is both a product and a provider of wise guidance, contributing to a vibrant, resilient, and progressive Africa.

Support For Cross-Border Mentorship

In our interconnected world, the notion of mentorship has transcended beyond local communities, reaching across borders to link diverse cultures and experiences. The digital era has significantly diminished geographical barriers, bringing about a profound opportunity to harness global wisdom through cross-border mentorship initiatives. These programs bring together diverse perspectives, enriching the mentorship experience by exposing mentors and mentees to a variety of insights and practices that only international collaboration can provide.

Imagine a young entrepreneur in Nairobi connected via a mentorship platform to a seasoned tech innovator in Silicon Valley. The exchange of ideas between such diverse locales could spark innovations that address local challenges with globally informed solutions. However, effective communication is key. Governments can facilitate this by supporting digital infrastructure improvements and advocating for policies that encourage digital literacy, ensuring that both mentors and mentees have the necessary tools and skills to engage effectively across digital platforms.

Financial transactions can be a hurdle in cross-border mentorship, particularly when it involves funding or resource exchange. By simplifying these processes, perhaps through regulatory frameworks that support secure and straightforward digital payments, governments can remove a significant barrier to international mentorship engagement. This could involve establishing bilateral agreements that recognize and simplify the taxation of financial transactions made in the context of mentorship programs.

Policies that foster international cooperation are crucial. This might look like multinational agreements that facilitate mentorship exchanges, offering visas or travel grants to mentees and mentors who need to meet in person or attend international workshops and conferences. Such efforts not only enhance the mentorship experience but also foster a deeper cultural understanding and solidarity among participants from different backgrounds.

These policy efforts can turn the ideal of a globally connected mentorship network into a practical reality, enabling individuals across Africa—and indeed, around the world—to not only dream global but also act global. By supporting cross-border mentorship initiatives, we not only expand the horizons of what individuals can achieve but also contribute to a richer, more diverse global community where knowledge and wisdom flow freely across borders.

In envisioning a future where cross-border mentorship is commonplace, we are paving the way for unprecedented collaboration and innovation. This effort isn't just about sharing knowledge; it's about building a world where collective wisdom transcends boundaries, fostering global growth and understanding.

Personal Tax Incentives For Mentors

Picture this: a bustling marketplace of ideas and knowledge, where everyone, regardless of age, has something valuable to offer. Now, imagine if participating in this vibrant exchange could not only enrich your community but also bring personal benefits, like tax incentives. It's a compelling idea, right?

The concept is simple yet powerful: introduce tax incentives for individuals who dedicate their time to mentoring through formal programs. This policy would leverage the profound wisdom and experience found within every community, mobilizing it to foster the growth and development of the next generation.

Tax breaks for mentors would serve as a tangible acknowledgment and reward for their contributions. It would not just encourage more people to step forward as mentors but also underline the value that society places on passing down knowledge and nurturing future talent. Consider a mechanic with decades of experience or a retired teacher—each holds a treasure trove of insights and expertise. If these individuals could receive a tax reduction for formally sharing their skills with young apprentices or students, it wouldn't just benefit the mentees but also provide a financial boon to the mentors. This approach could significantly shift how we view education and skill-sharing, making it a community-centric activity that's supported and encouraged at all levels.

The ripple effects of such a policy could be profound. By incentivizing mentorship, we foster closer ties between generations, enhance practical education, and strengthen community bonds. This isn't just about reducing someone's tax bill—it's about investing in social capital and ensuring that valuable life lessons and professional wisdom are passed on. Implementing such a policy would require careful consideration—defining what qualifies as formal mentorship, ensuring the programs meet certain standards, and establishing a system to verify participation without creating cumbersome bureaucracy.

With a policy like this, every community member who has something to teach would not only be more willing but would be celebrated for stepping into a mentor's role. It's about creating a culture that celebrates lifelong learning and mutual growth. By embracing such policies, we not only enrich individual lives but also weave a tighter, more resilient social fabric that supports the growth of every community member. It's a vision where personal growth and societal development go hand in hand, supported by a framework that recognizes and rewards the pivotal role of mentorship.

In this envisioned future, the act of mentoring becomes a recognized and valued contribution to society. Imagine communities where the wisdom of elders is actively sought and cherished, where professionals see mentoring not as an extra task but as a valued part of their civic duty, rewarded and acknowledged by society. This could create a virtuous cycle of continuous learning and teaching, making knowledge transfer a cornerstone of community life.

This approach could transform how we perceive and engage in mentorship, making it an integral part of our social and economic fabric. It's a win-win scenario—mentors receive financial benefits, mentees gain invaluable knowledge and skills, and communities grow stronger and more cohesive. This is not just a policy suggestion; it's a vision for a future where mentorship is celebrated and incentivized, ensuring that every generation has the opportunity to learn, grow, and contribute to the collective well-being.

Tax Incentives For Mentoring Businesses

Reflecting on the stories of countless businesses across Africa that have ventured into the world of mentorship, one can't help but imagine how significantly tax incentives could encourage more enterprises to take this commendable step. Envision a world where businesses are not just commercial entities but pillars of community growth and development, actively engaged in nurturing the next generation of professionals.

Picture that: a local tech startup decides to invest time in mentoring young tech enthusiasts. The company dedicates hours each week, providing hands-on training, guidance, and support. Now, imagine if this considerable investment of time and resources could be offset by tax breaks or reductions. This isn't just a cost-saving measure; it's a catalyst for change.

Under such a policy, businesses could receive tax credits directly proportional to the hours spent on mentoring activities or for hosting internships and practical training sessions as part of recognized mentorship initiatives. This approach would not only alleviate the financial burden on these companies but also provide a robust incentive for them to invest even more deeply in these programs.

The beauty of such a tax incentive lies in its simplicity and its potential impact. By lowering the fiscal responsibility of participating businesses, governments can transform corporate mentorship from a goodwill gesture into a financially viable and attractive proposition. Companies, both large and small, could see this as an opportunity to contribute to their communities while also benefiting from a tax perspective.

In this vision, tax incentives become more than just a financial relief; they become a tool for fostering corporate responsibility and community engagement. As businesses participate more actively in mentorship, they not only contribute to the professional growth of their mentees but also enrich their corporate culture, attract talent, and improve their public image.

Imagine the ripple effect in an economy where the private sector is deeply involved in shaping the workforce of tomorrow. This could drastically shift the landscape of employment and innovation in Africa, creating a more skilled, more adaptable, and more engaged workforce ready to take on the challenges of the future.

This is more than just a policy recommendation; it's a call to action for a sustainable partnership between the public and private sectors, a strategy that promises to empower not just individuals but entire communities, driving a wave of socioeconomic development across the continent.

Empowering Change: Envisioning A National Mentorship Program Managed By Ngos

In a place like my country, where the culture of mentorship hasn't blossomed as robustly as in other parts of Africa, I often daydream about a national mentorship program, which I have been thinking of proposing as a policy. But I think it still needs profound reflection to refine it. It's a vision that places the government in a pivotal role—not to manage but to enable. Here's how I see it unfolding:

Empowering NGOs to Lead: The government's role should be to catalyze the creation of a national mentorship program by funding and supporting it, but it should hand the reins over to NGOs to run it. NGOs are typically closer to the community and understand the unique challenges and needs of the local population better than government agencies might. They are often more agile and innovative in their approaches, which is essential in a program that requires adaptation and personalization.

Government Funding: One of the biggest hurdles, of course, is funding. It's hard to imagine, yet it's crucial. The government could allocate funds specifically for this cause, recognizing mentorship as a vital tool for national development. This funding would ensure the program's sustainability and allow it to reach a broad audience without financial constraints.

Training Bureaucrats as Mentors: An intriguing aspect of this plan is involving government bureaucrats as mentors. Every bureaucrat should receive training to become a mentor. This initiative could serve multiple purposes: it would develop the bureaucrats' leadership and empathetic skills, bridge the gap between government and citizens, and ensure that the values of public service permeate through community interactions.

Volunteerism Among Citizens: Beyond the bureaucrats, this program would encourage citizens from all walks of life to step forward as mentors. By volunteering, individuals from various professions and backgrounds could share their knowledge and experiences, enriching the mentorship pool.

Creating a Culture of Mentorship: The ultimate goal of such a program isn't just to guide the youth but to foster a widespread culture of mentorship. This would mean transforming mentorship from a formal arrangement into a fundamental part of societal interaction, where knowledge and wisdom are freely exchanged, and where every individual feels both empowered and responsible to contribute to the community's well-being.

I think this vision for a national mentorship program, supported by government funding but led by NGOs and fueled by the participation of bureaucrats and citizens alike, could significantly shift the mentoring landscape in my country. It's about building a future where mentorship is not an exception but a norm, embedded in the very fabric of our societal structure.

However, there are some concerns we need to address to make this vision a reality. First, while NGOs are generally closer to the communities, there's always the risk of varying quality and accountability. Not all NGOs operate at the same level of efficiency or effectiveness, and without proper oversight, the program could suffer from inconsistency. To overcome this, we could establish a standardized framework for all participating NGOs. This would include clear guidelines, performance metrics, and regular evaluations to ensure consistency and high standards. A central coordinating body could oversee the implementation and monitor progress, ensuring that all NGOs adhere to the set standards.

Funding is another major hurdle. Relying solely on government funding can be precarious, given the many competing priorities and potential for budget cuts. Instead, we could adopt a mixed funding model that includes partnerships with the private sector, international donors, and philanthropic foundations. Creating a dedicated mentorship fund where various stakeholders can contribute would diversify funding sources and provide financial stability, reducing the risk of interruptions due to budgetary constraints.

Involving government bureaucrats as mentors is a fascinating idea, but it comes with its own set of challenges. Bureaucrats might lack the time, motivation, or skills needed for effective mentoring. Participation should be voluntary and incentivized. We could offer professional development credits, recognition, and other benefits to motivate bureaucrats to engage fully. Additionally, providing them with comprehensive training tailored to their roles and responsibilities would ensure they are well-prepared for mentorship.

Another critical aspect is ensuring the program's reach and inclusivity. Volunteerism among citizens from all walks of life is essential. To manage this effectively, we need a robust volunteer management system. This would involve thorough recruitment processes, regular training sessions, and continuous support for volunteers. Implementing a mentorship platform to match mentors and mentees based on interests and skills can also enhance the program's effectiveness. Recognizing and rewarding volunteers for their contributions can help retain them and maintain high levels of engagement.

A significant challenge is creating a culture where mentorship is deeply valued and integrated into everyday life. This cultural shift requires a multifaceted approach, including public awareness campaigns, community events, and integration into educational curricula. Highlighting success stories and the tangible benefits of mentorship through various media channels can inspire more people to participate. Partnering with influential community leaders and organizations can also help embed the culture of mentorship more deeply into society.

As I envision this national mentorship program, I see it as more than just a series of formal arrangements. It's about creating an environment where mentorship becomes a fundamental part of societal interaction. Imagine a community where every individual feels both empowered and responsible to contribute to the community's well-being through mentorship. This vision involves strategic planning, collaboration, and a commitment to overcoming the challenges that arise.

By addressing these potential hurdles with thoughtful solutions, we can build a robust and sustainable mentorship ecosystem. This approach will enhance individual growth, community development, and pave the way for a brighter and more empowered future for our country. It's about ensuring that the seeds of mentorship we plant today will grow into strong trees that provide shade and fruit for generations to come.

Reflecting on the breadth and potential of the policy recommendations outlined in this chapter, I think it becomes clear that mentorship is more than just an educational tool; it's a transformative force capable of reshaping the economic and social landscape of Africa. These policies, if embraced and implemented effectively, hold the key to unlocking a future where African entrepreneurs and young leaders flourish under the guidance of robust mentorship programs.

Imagine a future where these policies are not just ideas but active components of Africa's developmental strategy. In such a future, mentorship transcends its traditional boundaries, becoming a pivotal element in nurturing the continent's human capital. By establishing sustainable funding models, offering tax incentives, mandating corporate mentorship, and fostering an environment that values and recognizes mentorship, we lay down a solid foundation for growth and innovation.

The vision of expanding mentorship through cross-border collaborations and integrating it into national educational systems underlines a commitment to not just national but continental upliftment. It's a vision where mentorship is universally accessible, and every young African, like Amina, is provided the support to transform innovative ideas into reality, contributing positively to their communities and the broader global economy.

This ambitious blueprint for the future of mentorship in Africa hinges on the collaborative efforts of governments, private sector players, educational institutions, and international partners. Their combined commitment is crucial for turning these policy recommendations into actions that will fuel Africa's growth.

In conclusion, the potential of mentorship to drive significant change is immense. By adopting and implementing these comprehensive policy strategies, African nations can ensure that mentorship serves as a cornerstone of not just individual development but also as a critical driver of broader economic and societal progress. The future we envision is one of empowered leaders and innovators who are well-equipped to navigate the challenges of the modern world and lead Africa toward a prosperous and sustainable future.

CALL OF COMMITMENT

As we turn the final pages of our exploration into the expansive world of mentorship in Africa, we find ourselves at a significant crossroads. The journey thus far has revealed the immense power of mentorship to ignite change, foster growth, and nurture future leaders across the continent. Yet, the full realization of this potential hinges on a profound commitment —a collective dedication from everyone involved, from grassroots activists to governmental leaders.

In this concluding chapter, "Call of Commitment," I invite you to join a united effort to elevate and solidify the role of mentorship as a foundational pillar for development in Africa. This is not merely a recapitulation of what mentorship can accomplish; it is an urgent call to action, a plea for all of us to engage actively and wholeheartedly in nurturing the seeds of mentorship that have been planted.

The essence of our collective call to commitment is the understanding that mentorship is not just an individual act of guidance—it's a communal investment in our collective future. It challenges each one of us—whether policymakers, educators, entrepreneurs, or community leaders—to affirm our commitment to this cause. We must step up, not only to support mentorship initiatives but to actively participate in them, ensuring they grow, thrive, and multiply across our diverse communities.

This chapter aims to galvanize a movement, urging all stakeholders to harness their resources, knowledge, and networks to foster an environment where mentorship is revered as a crucial element of societal advancement and personal development. The actions we advocate for here are not mere suggestions; they are imperative steps that require robust collaboration, sustained effort, and an unwavering belief in the transformative impact of mentorship.

As we conclude, let this chapter serve as a clarion call to all who believe in Africa's potential and the transformative power of mentorship. Let us commit to a future where every young person on the continent has access to the mentorship needed to thrive and lead. This is our shared responsibility and, perhaps, the most important legacy we can leave for future generations. Together, let's pledge to make mentorship a cornerstone of Africa's vibrant and prosperous tomorrow.

A Call To Action For Mentors And Stakeholders

As we reach the end of our exploration of mentorship in Africa, we find ourselves at a defining moment. This isn't just the end of a discussion; it's the beginning of an action-driven commitment to shaping the future. Today, I extend a heartfelt call to every individual and organization to actively engage in mentorship initiatives. This is more than a plea for involvement—it's a rallying cry for a transformative movement that hinges on our collective efforts to empower and uplift the next generation of African leaders.

At the core of mentorship lies the transformative power of active participation. Every act of mentorship, whether offering guidance as a mentor, supporting as a financier, or advocating as a community leader, plants seeds of change. It's about believing in the potential of Africa's youth and investing in that belief through direct action. The effectiveness of these efforts is magnified when we all commit—every interaction, no matter how small, creates ripples that extend across the fabric of society.

Diversity enriches mentorship. The involvement of mentors from various backgrounds and experiences brings invaluable perspectives to the mentees, broadening their understanding of the world and enhancing their ability to navigate complex paths. This diversity not only enhances the mentorship experience but also promotes inclusivity, ensuring that mentees from all walks of life can see reflections of their potential in their mentors. Here, the call is for everyone, regardless of field or background, to bring their knowledge and experience to the mentorship table.

The sustainability of mentorship programs relies heavily on robust support systems. This is a direct appeal to organizations, businesses, and government entities to bolster their backing for these initiatives. Support is multifaceted—it's not just about funding. It includes providing training for mentors, developing robust mentorship programs, and establishing policies that facilitate and reward mentoring efforts. This structured support is crucial for expanding the scope and impact of mentorship initiatives, ensuring they are equipped to thrive and grow.

This call to action is a beacon for us all. It guides us toward a future where mentorship is a foundational element of societal development, woven into the very fabric of our daily interactions and institutional practices. By engaging actively, embracing diversity, and providing unwavering support, we can collectively propel the mentorship movement to new heights, ensuring that it remains a powerful force for positive change across Africa. Let's commit to this vision, working together to foster a continent of empowered leaders and innovators, ready to face the challenges of tomorrow and seize the opportunities that come their way.

The Path Forward: Commitment And Responsibility

As I reflect on the journey of mentorship across Africa, the path forward is marked by a resolute commitment and a profound responsibility. This journey isn't just about maintaining the momentum of existing mentorship initiatives; it's about forging a foundation for a future where mentorship is woven into the fabric of society, becoming a way of life.

Building sustainable models is crucial. The key to lasting mentorship programs lies in our collective commitment—where mentors, mentees, organizations, and governments come together to create frameworks that are resilient and adaptable over time. These models need to be versatile, designed to grow and evolve with the shifting landscapes of society, and resilient enough to stand firm against the inevitable challenges ahead. We need to build programs with clear, measurable goals and scalable strategies, ensuring they are equipped for both the present and the future. These initiatives must balance financial viability with cultural sensitivity and technological advancement to truly sustain their impact for generations to come.

My vision for Africa is a continent where mentorship permeates every community and sector. Mentorship should not be seen as an elite or isolated activity but as a universal norm—a core component of our societal DNA. This involves nurturing a culture where the value of mentorship is universally recognized and embraced, where people eagerly assume roles as both mentors and mentees. This cultural shift would encourage a continual exchange of knowledge and experience, enriching communities and empowering individuals across diverse backgrounds. The responsibility to cultivate such a culture extends beyond specific programs to include schools, corporations, and government policies, integrating mentorship into the fabric of daily life.

What legacy will our commitment to mentorship leave? I see a future where the mentees of today become the mentors of tomorrow, passing on the wisdom and support they received. This generational passing of the torch will ensure that the principles and benefits of mentorship endure, creating a self-sustaining cycle of growth and empowerment. This is the legacy we aim to build—a legacy where each successive generation enriches the next, contributing to a continuous cycle of development and community strength.

This path forward for mentorship in Africa calls for a united effort to nurture and expand mentorship initiatives. By committing to sustainable development, fostering a pervasive culture of mentorship, and focusing on the enduring legacy of our efforts, we can ensure that mentorship remains a pivotal force in shaping Africa's future. It is a commitment to the next generation—a pledge to foster an environment where every individual has the opportunity to grow, lead, and innovate, underpinned by the supportive hand of mentorship. Together, let's embrace this call to action and invest in a future that celebrates the rich potential and vibrant spirit of Africa.

As we reach the culmination of our journey through the exploration of mentorship in Africa, it's evident that what lies ahead is not just a continuation of efforts, but a call to deepen our collective commitment. This final chapter, far from being an end, heralds the dawn of a concerted movement—a clarion call to all who believe in the transformative power of mentorship.

Throughout this discussion, we've unpacked the myriad ways in which mentorship serves as a powerful catalyst for personal growth, societal change, and the nurturing of Africa's future leaders. Yet, the true potency of mentorship hinges on the active involvement and unwavering dedication of each one of us—mentors, stakeholders, communities, and beyond. This isn't just an invitation; it's a summons to step beyond conventional roles and contribute to a thriving mentorship ecosystem.

The charge before us is clear and shared. It's about more than offering guidance—it's about investing in the foundations that will empower the next generation of Africans to lead with innovation, integrity, and insight. By embedding a culture of mentorship deeply within the fabric of daily life, we pave the way not only for sustainable development and gender equality but for a society rich in cooperation and compassion.

This chapter closes with a profound invitation to each of us to join in this transformative journey. It's a call to weave mentorship into every layer of African society, nurturing the leaders, thinkers, and visionaries of tomorrow. As we embrace this call with commitment and passion, we commit to a future where mentorship is not just present but is a pivotal cornerstone of a thriving Africa.

Let this not be just a conclusion to a text but the beginning of an actionable commitment from each of us. Let's rally together—educators, policymakers, entrepreneurs, and citizens—to champion mentorship as a vital tool for crafting a future as rich and vibrant as the continent itself. Embrace this call with enthusiasm and dedication, and together, let's build an Africa that shines brightly, propelled by the power of its people united in mentorship.

CONCLUSION

Mentorship is a powerful catalyst for social change, particularly in Africa, where it holds the potential to shape the future of generations. This book has explored the multifaceted impact of mentorship, highlighting its role in addressing a wide range of socio-economic and educational challenges. From historical perspectives to present-day applications, mentorship in Africa has evolved, demonstrating both formal and informal approaches that provide crucial support in areas such as academic achievement, career guidance, and overcoming barriers to education and employment. In an era where technology is rapidly transforming societies, leveraging digital platforms for mentorship has emerged as a pivotal strategy, enhancing accessibility and effectiveness.

The discussion on optimal ages for mentorship underscores the importance of timely intervention. Engaging youth at the right stages of their development ensures they receive the guidance necessary to navigate their educational and professional journeys successfully. Similarly, empowering individuals to become mentors at appropriate times in their lives fosters a culture of giving back and community support. Addressing physical and mental health challenges through mentorship programs has also been a significant focus. Promoting healthy relationships and support systems contributes to the overall well-being of individuals, making them better equipped to contribute positively to society. The incorporation of health-focused mentorship initiatives illustrates the holistic approach needed to tackle these issues.

Furthermore, mentorship programs require robust recruitment and retention strategies, adequate funding, and resource allocation to ensure their sustainability and impact. Overcoming cultural and societal barriers, ensuring program quality, and leveraging technology are critical components in creating effective and enduring mentorship networks. The role of government, NGOs, and the private sector in supporting mentorship initiatives cannot be overstated. Collaborative efforts are essential in building networks that provide the necessary resources and opportunities for mentorship programs to thrive. Case studies of successful government-backed initiatives highlight the benefits of such collaborations, illustrating their positive impact on societal development and stability.

As we draw the final lines of this exploration into the vibrant world of mentorship in Africa, we find ourselves enveloped in a narrative that's as compelling as it is transformative. This book is more than a collection of chapters; it's a vivid tapestry woven from stories of change, development, and empowerment through mentorship—a testament to its potential as a profound agent for societal transformation across the continent. Reflecting on the role of African governments and the diaspora, it becomes clear that their involvement is indispensable. Governments have the capacity to enact policies that foster a conducive environment for mentorship, while the diaspora can offer a wealth of knowledge and resources, bridging gaps and enriching mentorship experiences with global insights. Their collaboration is key to unlocking the full potential of Africa's youth, propelling them toward the opportunities that await in their futures.

The stories shared—of young entrepreneurs, aspiring leaders, and communities transformed—illustrate the profound impact mentorship can have. Each narrative underscores the importance of sustained commitment and shared responsibility. By fostering a culture where mentorship is valued and supported, we pave the way for a future where every African has the chance to thrive. This final chapter is not just a summary but a call to action— a plea for continued commitment to the mentorship movement. It's an invitation to everyone, from policymakers to educators, and from business leaders to community members, to play a part in this transformative journey.

The path forward is clear. With collective effort and unwavering dedication, mentorship can continue to be a cornerstone of development in Africa. Let this book serve as a beacon, inspiring each of us to take part in nurturing and expanding the reach of mentorship programs. Together, we can ensure that the legacy of mentorship is not only preserved but also strengthened, blossoming into a force that drives Africa toward a future rich with opportunity, equality, and enduring social progress.

In embracing this call, we not only commit to supporting the current generation but also to laying a foundation for those to come. Let us move forward with the resolve that our actions today will echo through the lives of future generations, cementing mentorship as a pivotal element in Africa's vibrant tapestry of growth and success. Mentorship is not merely an initiative; it is a movement that has the power to reshape societies. As we continue to champion this cause, let us remember that every mentor-mentee relationship is a step toward a brighter, more inclusive future. By investing in the potential of our youth, we invest in the potential of our continent. This is our moment to act, to build, and to inspire. Let us seize it with both hands, ensuring that the spirit of mentorship thrives in every corner of Africa, driving us all toward a horizon filled with promise and possibility.

GLOSSARY

Mentorship - a developmental relationship where a more experienced or knowledgeable person helps to guide a less experienced or knowledgeable person. Mentorship involves providing advice, sharing knowledge, and offering emotional support to foster the personal and professional growth of the mentee.

Mentee - an individual who receives guidance, knowledge, and support from a mentor. Mentees are often seeking to gain skills, improve their capabilities, and advance their careers or personal development through the mentorship relationship.

Social Change - significant alterations over time in behavior patterns, cultural values and norms, and social structures. Social change is often aimed at improving societal conditions and can be driven by individuals, organizations, or movements.

Sustainable Development - development that meets the needs of the present without compromising the ability of future generations to meet their own needs. It encompasses a broad range of economic, social, and environmental objectives.

Empowerment - the process of becoming stronger and more confident, especially in controlling one's life and claiming one's rights. Empowerment involves increasing the decision-making power of individuals or groups, enhancing their ability to influence societal structures.

Cultural Competence - the ability to understand, appreciate, and interact with people from cultures or belief systems different from one's own. Cultural competence involves being aware of one's own world view, avoiding cultural assumptions, and respecting differences.

Leadership - the act of guiding or influencing a group towards a goal or vision. Leadership involves setting direction, inspiring others, and fostering an environment where individuals can contribute effectively to achieving collective objectives.

Innovation - the process of translating an idea or invention into a good or service that creates value or for which customers will pay. Innovation involves deliberate application of information, imagination, and initiative in deriving greater or different values from resources.

Gender Equality - the state in which access to rights or opportunities is unaffected by gender. Gender equality involves the equal treatment of all genders, including the removal of barriers that result from gendered expectations and biases.

Social Entrepreneurship - the use of startup companies and other entrepreneurs to develop, fund, and implement solutions to social, cultural, or environmental issues. Social entrepreneurs combine business principles and social missions to generate both financial and social returns.

Digital Platforms - online tools and websites that facilitate the creation, sharing, and exchange of information, ideas, career interests, and other forms of expression via virtual communities and networks.

Data Analytics - the process of examining data sets in order to draw conclusions about the information they contain. Data analytics techniques and processes are used to enhance productivity and business gain.

Community Engagement - the process of working collaboratively with community groups to address issues that impact the well-being of those groups. It involves building lasting relationships based on mutual respect and trust.

Resilience - the capacity to recover quickly from difficulties, toughness. In the context of individuals and communities, resilience refers to the ability to withstand and bounce back from challenges and adversities.

Mentor Training Modules - structured educational resources designed to equip mentors with the necessary skills, knowledge, and attitudes to effectively support their mentees. These modules often cover topics such as communication, goal setting, and feedback delivery.

Mentee Preparation Guides - instructional materials aimed at helping mentees maximize their mentorship experience. These guides typically include tips on setting personal objectives, engaging in productive dialogues with mentors, and applying learned insights.

Funding Models - various strategies and sources for securing financial support for mentorship programs. This includes grants, donations, sponsorships, and partnerships with private and public entities.

Program Evaluation - the systematic assessment of the processes and outcomes of a program to determine its effectiveness, impact, and areas for improvement. Evaluation methods can be qualitative, quantitative, or a mix of both.

Templates and Tools - standardized documents and resources that assist in the planning, execution, and assessment of mentorship programs. These may include mentor and mentee application forms, agreement templates, and evaluation checklists.

Cultural Competence Resources - educational materials and programs designed to enhance individuals' ability to understand, communicate with, and effectively interact with people across cultures.

Sustainable Development Goals (SDGs) - a collection of 17 global goals set by the United Nations General Assembly in 2015 for the year 2030. The SDGs aim to address global challenges, including those related to poverty, inequality, climate change, environmental degradation, peace, and justice.

Diversity - the inclusion of individuals from a wide range of backgrounds and experiences, including but not limited to races, ethnicities, genders, ages, religions, disabilities, and sexual orientations.

Inclusive Mentorship - mentorship programs designed to be accessible and beneficial to a diverse group of participants, taking into account various backgrounds, experiences, and needs to ensure equitable opportunities for growth and development.

Empathetic Leadership - a leadership style that emphasizes understanding, compassion, and putting oneself in others' shoes to lead and make decisions that consider the wellbeing and perspectives of all stakeholders.

Cross-Sector Collaboration - partnerships between different sectors of society, including the public sector, private sector, and civil society, to address complex challenges through combining resources, expertise, and efforts.

Digital Divide - the gap between individuals and communities that have access to modern information and communication technology and those that do not or have restricted access. This divide can impact access to information, education, and opportunities.

Environmental Stewardship - responsible use and protection of the natural environment through conservation and sustainable practices. It involves individuals and organizations committing to the preservation of natural resources for future generations.

Social Innovation - the development and implementation of novel solutions to social problems that are more effective, efficient, sustainable, or just than current solutions. Social innovation can occur within governments, businesses, or nonprofits, as well as within communities.

Empowerment Strategies - methods and approaches used to increase the degree of autonomy and self-determination in people and communities to enable them to represent their interests in a responsible and self-determined way, acting on their own authority.

Capacity Building - the process of developing and strengthening the skills, instincts, abilities, processes, and resources that organizations and communities need to survive, adapt, and thrive in a fast-changing world.

Sustainable Practices - actions and initiatives that meet the needs of the present without compromising the ability of future generations to meet their own needs, particularly concerning environmental preservation and social responsibility.

Mentor Training - programs and workshops designed to equip potential mentors with the necessary skills, knowledge, and attitudes to effectively guide and support their mentees.

Interdisciplinary Approach - combining or involving two or more academic disciplines or fields of study to explore topics, issues, or questions from multiple perspectives. In mentorship, it involves drawing on diverse fields to provide a holistic support system for mentees.

Virtual Mentoring - the process of conducting mentorship activities through digital means, such as video calls, messaging apps, and online platforms, allowing for mentorship relationships to flourish despite physical distance.

Peer Mentoring - a form of mentorship that occurs between individuals who are similar in age, experience, or position, where peers support each other's growth and development through shared experiences and mutual guidance.

Cross-Cultural Mentoring - a mentorship relationship involving mentors and mentees from different cultural backgrounds, emphasizing the learning and exchange of cultural insights and fostering global understanding and respect.

Youth Engagement - the meaningful participation and sustained involvement of a young person in an activity or initiative with a focus outside of themselves, often linked to personal growth, skill development, or social change.

Social Entrepreneurship - the practice of identifying, starting, and growing successful mission-driven businesses and innovations that strive to solve social problems and benefit society.

Leadership Development - programs or activities that aim to enhance the leadership qualities and capabilities of individuals, preparing them for roles that involve guiding, influencing, or managing others.

Mentorship Ecosystem - dynamic network or community that supports the growth and development of mentorship relationships, including individuals, organizations, resources, and cultural elements that contribute to the effectiveness and sustainability of mentorship.

Digital Literacy - the ability to find, evaluate, utilize, share, and create content using information technologies and the Internet. In mentorship, it encompasses equipping mentees with the skills to navigate digital platforms effectively.

Gender Sensitivity - the recognition and understanding of the differences in gender roles and expectations, and the implementation of strategies to address and mitigate gender-based disadvantages or discrimination.

Feedback Mechanisms - systems or processes established within mentorship programs to collect and analyze feedback from mentors and mentees, aiming to improve the mentorship experience and outcomes based on participants' insights and suggestions.

Community Resilience - the ability of a community to adapt to and recover from adverse situations, such as economic downturns, natural disasters, or social disruptions, through effective planning, resource management, and collective action.

Entrepreneurial Mentorship - guidance and support provided by experienced entrepreneurs to individuals or groups starting new business ventures, focusing on building business skills, navigating challenges, and fostering innovation.

Corporate Social Responsibility (CSR) - a business model that helps a company be socially accountable—to itself, its stakeholders, and the public. CSR initiatives often support mentorship programs as part of a company's commitment to contributing positively to society.

Mentorship Networks - organized groups or associations that bring together mentors and mentees, facilitating connections, sharing resources, and fostering a supportive community for mentorship activities.

Social Capital - the networks, relationships, and norms that enable collective action and cooperation within a society. In mentorship, social capital refers to the value derived from social networks and the support and resources that come from them.

APPENDIX A

Become a Mentor and Mentee
https://sayesmentoring.org/mentors/

Become a Partner
https://sayesmentoring.org/non-profit-partners/

APPENDIX B

References And Further Reading

Books and Publications:

"How Effective are Mentoring Programs for Youth" - A detailed analysis on the efficacy of mentoring programs tailored for young individuals.

"How to Build a Successful Mentoring Program" - This guide offers insights into the critical elements that contribute to the success of mentoring programs.

"Hundred Ideas to Use When Mentoring Youth" - A resource providing a variety of actionable ideas to enhance the mentoring experience for youth.

"Improving Development Results Through Excellence in Evaluation" - Focuses on how robust evaluation practices can significantly improve the outcomes of developmental programs.

"Increasing Person-Centered Thinking" - Discusses strategies to center mentoring approaches around the personal needs and thoughts of the mentee.

"Leaving Care - John Pinkerton" - Discusses strategies for supporting youth transitioning out of care systems through mentoring.

"Mentorship in Higher Education: Practical Advice and Leadership Theories" by Kathy L. Jackson - A guide that offers insights into the theories and practices of mentorship in an educational context.

"African Business, Culture, and Politics: Insights for Business Success and Development" by Neal Knighton - This book provides an in-depth look at the business landscape in Africa, focusing on cultural and political factors that affect entrepreneurship and economic growth.

"The Role of Technology in Developing Entrepreneurs and Leaders" by Samantha Wade - An article that explores how technological advances are shaping leadership and entrepreneurial efforts in emerging economies, particularly in Africa.

"Sustainable Development Goals and African Societal

Transformation" by United Nations Publications - A comprehensive resource on how the SDGs are being implemented in Africa, with case studies on successful initiatives and recommendations for future efforts.

"Cross-Cultural Mentoring: A Pathway to Making Global Connections" by Linda Phillips-Jones, Ph.D. - Focuses on the impact of cross-cultural relationships in mentorship, providing practical advice on fostering effective international mentor-mentee relationships.

"Empowering Women Through Mentoring" by Sally Helgesen - This book discusses the specific benefits and strategies of mentorship for women, with applicability to the challenges faced by African women in business and leadership.

"Leadership and Management in Africa: A Cultural Perspective" by Terrence Jackson - An exploration of how cultural contexts influence management and leadership styles across Africa.

"Building Resilience in African Entrepreneurs" by John-Paul Iwuoha - An article detailing strategies for African entrepreneurs to build resilience and succeed in challenging economic environments.

Journals and Articles:

Mentorship and its impact on African entrepreneurship, Journal of African Business Development

The Role of Mentorship in Economic Empowerment, African Economic Review

Online Resources:

Publications from SAYes Mentoring

For those interested in the specific application of mentorship in transition services for youth, SAYes offers several insightful publications to which I have also contributed.

Mentoring Youth: Key Messages for Young People

Evaluating the Contribution of Formal Youth Mentoring

Implementing E-mentoring with Care-Experienced Youth Under 'Lock-Down'

SAYes Mentoring Resource Bank: Updated quarterly, this resource is invaluable for mentors and mentees in Africa looking for guidance and tools to navigate educational and career decisions. https://sayesmentoring.org/publications/

World Bank Group's Independent Evaluation Group (IEG) - Insights on evaluation practices that improve the impact of development programs, including mentoring.

Regional Centers for Learning on Evaluation and Results – A collaborative initiative enhancing evaluation skills globally.

Government and Institutional Reports:

Policy Framework for Mentorship Programs in Africa - A comprehensive report by the African Development Bank on implementing effective mentorship policies.

Guidelines for Cross-border Mentorship in Africa - An intergovernmental policy document facilitating mentorship across African borders.

These resources are complemented by various scholarly articles, case studies, and program evaluations available in academic journals and through mentorship organizations worldwide. Each entry not only supports the discussions found within the chapters of this book but also encourages ongoing engagement and action from all stakeholders involved in mentorship across Africa.